Peaks, Palms & Picnics

*Day Journeys in the Mountains & Deserts
of Palm Springs and the Coachella Valley
of Southern California*

Linda McMillin Pyle

Edited by
Evelyn Tschida McMillin

Sunbelt Publications
San Diego, CA

Peaks, Palms and Picnics
Sunbelt Publications
Copyright © 1999, 2002 by Linda McMillin Pyle
All rights reserved. Second Edition, 2002. Third printing, 2011.

Sunbelt Publications, Inc.
P.O. Box 191126
San Diego, CA 92159-1126
619-258-4911 • 619-258-4916 (fax)
www.sunbeltbooks.com

All photos by Linda McMillin Pyle unless otherwise credited
Cover photo, courtesy of Palm Springs Bureau of Tourism
www.palm-springs.org
Text design, layout, and composition by Silvercat®, San Diego, California
Updated edition by Leah Cooper

15 14 13 12 11   7 6 5 4 3

Library of Congress Cataloging-in-Publication Data
Pyle, Linda McMillin.
    Peaks, palms & picnics : day journeys in the mountains & deserts of Palm Springs and the Coachella Valley of Southern California / Linda McMillin Pyle ; edited by Evelyn Tschida McMillin.
        p. cm.
Updated ed. of: Peaks, palms, and picnics. Philadelphia : Xlibris Corp., c1999.
Includes bibliographical references and index.
    ISBN 0-916251-57-8
1. California, Southern—Guidebooks. 2. Palm Springs (Calif.)—Guidebooks.
3. Palm Springs Region (Calif.)—Guidebooks. 4. Coachella Valley (Calif.)—Guidebooks. 5. Hiking—California, Southern—Guidebooks. I. Title: Peaks, palms, and picnics. II.
McMillin, Evelyn Tschida. III. Title.
    F867 .P95 2002
    917.94'90454—dc21
                                                        2002003397

Printed in the United States of America

Contents

*Denotes Raw food recipe

Location of Journeys

Map Key

(See chapter travel notes for driving directions)

1 San Jacinto Peak Trail, Desert View Trail
2 Desert Museum & Trail
3 Palm Canyon Trail
4 Murray Canyon Trail
5 Andreas Canyon Trail
6 North end of South Lykken Trail
7 McCallum Adobe/Village Green
8 Downtown Palm Springs Walking Tour
9 North Lykken Trail
10 South Lykken Trail
11 Garstin Trail to Berns & Araby Trails
12 Downtown Strolling Tour
13 Bighorn Overlook Trail
14 Mirage Trail
15 Art Smith Trail
16 Living Desert Wildlife & Botanical Park
17 Toro and Santa Rosa Peaks

18 Pinyon Flats Trail
19 Cedar Spring/Jo Pond Trail to Garnet Ridge
20 Cahuilla Peak Trail
21 La Quinta Resort and Club, Bear Creek Canyon Trail
22 Boo Hoff Trail
23 Fish Traps, Travertine Rock
24 Date Garden Tour
25 Painted Canyon, & Salton Sea Recreational Area
26 General Patton Memorial Museum
26a Desert Flight Museum in Palm Springs
27 Dos Palmas Preserve
28 Wind Farm Tour
29 Whitewater Canyon, Rainbow Rancho Trout Farm
30 Coachella Valley Preserve
31 Big Morongo Canyon Trails
32 Joshua Tree National Park
33 Willie Boy Trail

Dear Readers,

It took me a few years to complete this updated and revised third printing because we were having so darn much fun doing the research. In fact so much fun, I couldn't fit all the new chapters inside this book so some have gone into an upcoming day journey book titled *Awesome Day Journeys-Palm Springs*.

I am proud to include in this printing of *Peaks, Palms and Picnics*, recipes from Michael Miller, a graduate of the Living Light Culinary Raw Food School in Fort Bragg, California. What could be better than healthy food combined with fun day journeys and hikes!

Since this book was last updated, the Cahuilla Mountain Wilderness has been designated, protecting 5,585 acres with spectacular views and preserving the fictional home of Helen Hunt Jackson's Alessandro and Ramona (detailed in Chapter 20, Trail of Romantic Old California in Ramona's Country). These chaparral covered slopes and forested mountaintop are home to mountain lion, quail and the rare red diamond rattlesnake. And the Wildlands Conservancy Whitewater Preserve has been designated, as well, protecting 2,826 acres and adding some new spectacular hiking trails detailed in Chapter 29, Trail of Whitewater Canyon.

Since the 2nd edition of the book was published, we have put many miles on our feet. We walked the Wicklow Way in Ireland, the entire 100 miles of the West Highland Way in Scotland, over 60 miles in Alberta and Calgary, British Colombia, many miles of California trails in Napa, Sonoma, Mendocino County and in the Point Reyes National Seashore. Last summer, we spent a week hiking between hill towns in Tuscany, Italy. Mama Mia, that was a peak walking experience (and an upcoming book) but I always return to walking this desert which is my greatest source of joy and inspiration. (It is also the setting for my historical fiction book, *Dawn Breaks in the West*.) And speaking of inspiration, the hardest thing for this update was that my parents were no longer able to walk with us but their past experiences still remain inside this edition.

And finally, I have come to understand, I'm not ever going to "get done" hiking this desert. I'm eager to see what is next. I hope you enjoy these journeys! They are my love letters to the desert.

Linda Pyle

A portion of the sale of this book will go to
Friends of the Desert Mountains and to The Living Desert.

To those Chroniclers Who Painted A Picture Of The Desert As It Was Around A Century Ago: Chief Francisco Patencio, J. Smeaton Chase, George Wharton James And Carl Eytel

To T.M. For Supporting This Project And Trail Mastering

To Mom For Endless Contributions And Editing

To Dad For Driving Many Miles And Contributing The Map

To Friends And Family For Encouragement Along The Trail

Introduction

Peaks, Palms & Picnics is the story of four travelers
ages forty to eighty years exploring and picnicking in the mountains and
deserts of Palm Springs and the Coachella Valley
highlighting thirty-three trails for adventure at any age

Trails and food shared with family and friends give a
deeper meaning to life
For each trail there are simple recipes—light meals in hand
for trailside picnics served alfresco on the peaks or under the palms
inspired by the first people of Agua Caliente, skilled
master-gathers of desert and woodland foods
and the nineteenth and early twentieth century pioneers
who introduced dates, fruits and vegetables to the Valley

Come to the oasis where fan palms flutter, cool and shade
See the real desert appear when you step off sidewalks
and green grass up to the granite peaks that rise above the
city or along sandy desert that stretches out invitingly

Trod ancient Native American footpaths
step into a Fish Trap under an age-old sea
Ride into the old West of the romantic stagecoach days
along the Bradshaw Trail
join the posse of the last organized manhunt of the West
or pound along the lonely journey of the last local Pony
Express Rider

Fire your imagination along the wilderness paths that were the
gateways to the American dream in the Far West

Sit beside the enigmatic blue Salton Sea and
let the colors of the Painted Canyon and Indian Canyons
seep deep inside
Experience the warm gentle brown of the restoring mountains
Observe the light changing on these powerful pyramids at
twilight when mountains lose their dimension and
become silhouettes pasted upon a skyline

Step along the path strewn with blooming yellow brittlebush
Walk the history trail of the pioneers of Palm Springs and
the writers and artists who passed along the same trails a century ago
Stroll the Palm Springs avenues that movie stars claimed as their own

Meet a smiling mountain lion named Reno and a
wayward Bighorn sheep called Rosie
Come along—jump in anywhere—
There is time for the swimming pool and the golf course
but first feast on the wilderness
drink from the soul of the desert
Find serendipity in unexpected surprises and delights
a traveler cannot plan
COME STEP INTO THE DESERT

Trail of San Jacinto Peak

Palm Springs Aerial Tramway ride to Long Valley, easy
Desert View walk or challenging hike to top of San Jacinto

&⁊ Omar's Bread

Awake! for Morning in the Bowl of Night
Has flung the Stone that puts the Stars to Flight:
And Lo! the Hunter of the East has caught
The Sultan's Turret in a Noose of Light
　　　　　　Edward Fitzgerald-translation

The first quatrain of the Rubaiyat of Omar Khayyam, the eleventh century astronomer-poet of the Persian desert, echoes on a high country trail in the San Jacinto wilderness on an early morning hike. The magnificent granite turret, Mount San Jacinto peak, with the boldest escarpment in North America, is the spire upon which the sun rises and sets so compellingly in this, our Colorado Desert. Forming a backdrop of incredible soaring heights for Palm Springs, now in summer the bald peak rises smoke gray. In spring, fingers of white gleam in rivers of snow. Winter brings a pinnacle of alabaster lending a sense of grandeur to all the surrounding land.

On our TRAIL OF THE SAN JACINTO PEAK, we are drawn up into the sky on this ageless mountain with its forever vistas of wilderness and endless desert. But first we must begin at the station.

Chino Valley Station

At the north edge of Palm Springs, Mom, Dad, my husband Scott and I follow Tramway Road climbing the alluvial fan to the Chino Canyon Valley Station at an elevation of 2,643 feet. Imposing sheer rock faces press down as we drive into an awesome canyon.

This canyon was once summer home to the Cahuilla Indians. Chief Francisco Patencio, a respected desert Cahuilla Indian often quoted on the history of the Coachella Valley, was born in Chino Canyon in the 1840s and died at about 100 years of age. He recalled the flat lands high in the canyon were good for fields and gardens but also in great peril during floods. He said his ancestors could take refuge here from the exploring Spaniards passing through the lower valley and later from the Californios, people born in California of Hispanic ancestry in the nineteenth century. Chino Canyon was hidden from the desert floor.

These early explorers were using an ancient Indian trade route that ran through the San Gorgonio Pass. Trade routes were important to the Cahuilla as luxury items such as food, shells, animal and mineral products were exchanged with Chumash and Gabrielino coastal tribes. Travelers carried important messages; they were the newspapers of the people. Like them, we have traveled from the coast not to trade goods but to trade moist ocean air for warm dry air of the desert.

Palm Springs Aerial Tram

A 14-minute vertical tram ride past five supporting towers whisks us up, up and away, ski lift fashion, past life zones not often seen stacked together horizontally. Enthralled, we stand at the rear window of the enclosed 80-passenger tram reveling in the exhilarating rise of the red car. Others with less affection for heights stand in the middle, eyes averted, concealing their trepidation.

Leaving the creosote and brittlebush of the desert, the tram travels past five geological life zones ranging from Sonoran to Arctic fringe and stops at the 8,516 foot mountain station with its gift shop, restaurant, snack bar and observation areas. A 22-minute movie on the history of the tram plays in the theater.

Stepping from the station into the cool forest, the scent of pines envelops us. The dry breeze blows now a comfortable 40 degrees cooler than on the valley floor.

Long Valley

Before entering the wilderness, we fill out day-use permits at the ranger station box at Long Valley, a short walk from the tram station. Long Valley with a short nature trail and a desert view trail invites with picnic tables and barbecue grills. Here, we part ways with Mom and Dad. Concerned about altitude changes, they will meander toward Round Valley staying in the flat of the valley. Scott, my husband and Trail Master, nicknamed T.M., and I are on a mission: lunch at the top of the Turret.

In the past, a hike into the high country for us was from the other side of the mountain. Then, bedraggled from a night in the tent and dusty from the trail, we met Palm Springs tram hikers in spotless white clothes and sandals with jaundiced eye. They seemed to be cheaters. Now, delivered by the same tram, fresh and ready to meet the challenge, it didn't seem so much like cheating as we still had an 11½ mile round trip to hike. Plus, Mom and Dad would be able to share the high country forest experience.

Round Valley

A march of two miles to Round Valley begins our ascent. T.M., always alert to signs of animals, spots several bushy-tailed coyotes. Eyes glowing in the dark forest, observing curiously, they remind that this is their wilderness, too.

Once these forests were the habitat of the most dangerous animal the Indians encountered, the grizzly bear. Like the bald eagle, the bear was sacred and not hunted. With difficulty and foreboding the Cahuilla men would ascend into the mountains with bows made of mesquite or desert willow: then descend, deer slung over shoulders, down through the steep cactus and chaparral infested slopes. This may have been a fearful task for them as the mountaintop was also the realm of the ubiquitous evil spirit, Tahquitz. With a penchant for stealing souls and concealing himself as solid rock, he could also appear in angry thunder and lightning or travel in frightful whirling dust devils.

No thunderclaps or lightening strikes as we reach a stream, our last chance to filter water. A trip to the outhouse is fast as spiders and bees have claimed it as their own. From Round Valley, we climb the trail past the sign marked "San Jacinto Peak."

San Jacinto Peak Trail

Our pace picks up after resting in the shade of lodgepole pines at Wellmans Divide, the junction of the Saddle Junction Trail and San Jacinto Peak Trail. The San Jacinto Peak Trail turns right. Soon we find ourselves out of the stately pine forest and into the bright sun on dry slopes switchbacking through an elfin forest of manzanita bushes. Branches and berries crown this large evergreen with its red-dish-brown twisted trunks. Manzanita means "little apple" in Spanish and the mealy berries are eaten by wildlife and were made into a cider by the Indians.

Soon we meet the Summit Trail and other hikers with the same destination. Pressing on, closer to the top of the mountain, a stone shelter built by the Civilian Conservation Corps in the 1930s provides emergency shelter.

A scramble up boulders advances us another 300 yards to the "top of the world." No peaked pinnacle to inspire or awe, it is a conglomeration of gigantic granite boulders balancing one atop the other creating this "summit of the exalted mountain."

> *Here with a Loaf of Bread beneath the bough,*
> *A flask of Wine, a book of Verse—and Thou*
> *Beside me singing in the Wilderness—*
> *And Wilderness is Paradise enow.*

From this elevated place, the pale purple horizon circumscribes the wilderness and our paradise. Our wine is thirst-quenching water, our bread is eaten next to a windswept limber pine tree and a travel journal is our book of verse.

An eagle's vista, a wide panning view, spots the mighty San Gorgonio peak, old "Greyback," the highest peak in Southern California. The 10,000-foot precipitous drop of a perpendicular escarpment falls away into thin air before us. This, the northeast face of San Jacinto Peak, is recognized as the most severe escarpment in North America.

Palm Springs and the Coachella Valley cities string out below on the tawny floor of the Colorado Desert. Disappearing in a haze, the Colorado Desert reaches eastward almost 250 miles to Phoenix and southward slips past the blue Salton Sea into northern Baja California and the Mexican state of Sonora.

In the deep western distance, the Pacific Ocean gleams only on a rare clear day. The Little San Bernardino Mountains to the northeast rise dim blue with a gilding of gold. Hidden behind them are the Mohave Desert and Joshua Tree National Park. The Santa Rosa Mountains to the south and southeast with windswept ridges stand out in sharp relief.

Our vistas and visions of the desert and mountains along many of the trails of the Coachella Valley would have belonged to Cahuilla Indian, Spanish explorer, Californio or American pioneer. These paths, worn by the feet of many travelers, mark places where visitors cannot now remain. In the year 2000, Congress created the Santa Rosa and San Jacinto Mountains National Monument, a patchwork of National Forests, State and Federal Wilderness, Indian reservations and Bureau of Land Management land. This enhanced the protection of 272,000 acres of land. Perhaps, someday in the future development will string all the way to Arizona but foresight and cooperation will have preserved some of this unique Western landscape.

The sudden rise to a high altitude and the hike begins to blur the senses and returning down the trail, legs straining, toes jamming, the last mile seems endless. Exhausted, collapsed on the waiting room floor at the mountain station, we are thankful the tram will keep us from having to descend another 6,000 feet on foot. I describe this hike as long, long and arduous, T.M. as a piece of cake. We are anxious to know how Mom and Dad fared in their ramblings.

Desert View Trail

They are not worn out but have a story to tell. Starting confidently up the Round Valley Trail behind us, talking and laughing, they proceeded until Mom spied six or seven coyotes slinking along on their own trail. With an abrupt about face, with fearless leader Mom leading the retreat, they exchanged their scant knowledge of what to do when facing a

Palm Springs Aerial Tramway
Courtesy of Palm Springs Bureau of Tourism

coyote pack—stand tall and not run? Or was that for mountain lions? They weren't exactly running but when they chanced upon a ranger and described their encounter, he had smiled. Seems the coyotes here are looked upon as merely part of the scenery.

Heartened by this news, they headed out again, this time on the 1½ mile Desert View Trail, an easy loop, pleasant with a slight rise to the brink of an escarpment dropping abruptly to the desert floor. After scenery gazing and resting among giant boulders, they proceeded close to the rim to another lookout with a similar spectacular viewpoint and then back down the easy slope to the picnic table area of Long Valley. Their adventures on the mountain and ours tell us that whether you are forty or eighty years old, time is fleeting.

Take Heed! Time Fleets Fast Away
Forty or Seventy, Dark Shadowed Forests beckon Stay
Share Together the Mystifying Mountain Air
Soon the Fall shuts Another Day

Travel notes

The Valley Station is located in north Palm Springs. From Highway 111 turn up Tramway Road and proceed 3½ miles to the station.

Admission fees: $23.25 adults, $21.25 seniors, $16.25 children ages 3-12. AAA discount applies. Information: www.pstramway.com or 760-325-1391. Check for closures due to weather or maintenance.

The easy Desert View loop is 1.5 miles and takes approximately 1 hour. Kids can become Junior Rangers. Stop by the Visitor Center on the mountain to get the fun details.

The strenuous hike to the San Jacinto peak is 11.5 miles roundtrip, 2400 feet of elevation gain and takes 5-7 hours. The limited water available must be filtered before use.

Wear comfortable walking shoes or hiking boots and bring plenty of water for longer hike to top. Be prepared for 40-degree temperature change from the desert floor. Day hikers should fill out a day pass at the Long Valley Ranger Station before starting the wilderness trails. Maps available in Long Valley and there is a picnic area with barbecue stoves and picnic tables.

Omar's Bread

1 package fast rise yeast
3½–4 cups flour
1¼ cup lukewarm water, divided
1 teaspoon salt
1/8 cup olive oil
Pinch of sugar
Cornmeal

- Dissolve salt and sugar in ¼ cup lukewarm water. Place 3 cups flour on breadboard. Make 6 inch well in center leaving some flour on bottom. Add yeast to sugar and salt water.
- Pour olive oil and yeast mixture into well. Start working flour into well gradually adding remaining 1 cup lukewarm water. Continue working flour toward center until a soft dough forms. Add more or less additional flour to form a ball.
- Knead dough 20 minutes on very lightly floured board picking up edges and folding to center, pushing dough away from you with heels of hands. Rotate dough ¼ turn and continue kneading until ball is smooth and elastic.
- Place in large greased bowl turning dough to grease all sides. Cover bowl with a cloth and allow to rise in a warm draft-free place such as an oven. To warm oven, heat at 200 degrees for 3–4 minutes and turn OFF. Allow to rise until double in bulk.
- Punch dough down with fist. Form into 4 balls. Place balls in greased bowl and return to oven allowing dough to rise 30 minutes.
- Lightly sprinkle cornmeal on two ungreased heavy baking sheets. On a lightly floured board, roll balls with rolling pin into 8 x 1/8 inch rounds.

Place rounds on baking sheets 2–3 inches apart. Cover with cloth and let rest 30 minutes.

- Preheat oven to 500 degrees Fahrenheit. Bake one pan at a time on lower rack for 3 minutes until loaf rises. Transfer to rack 3–4 inches higher. Continue baking 3 minutes more until light brown. Remove from oven. Immediately seal bread in aluminum foil wrapping tightly. Let rest 10 minutes. Serves 8.
- Serve warm or at room temperature. For the trail, pack cheese, peanut butter and jelly or fruit.

Trail of Inspiration

*Palm Springs Desert Museum and
challenging Museum Trail Hike*

❧ Greek Muses Tapenade Sandwich

The Muses, nine daughters of Zeus, were created to sing for the gods.
Clio, Urania, Thalia, Terpsichore, Calliope, Erato, Euterpe,
Polyhymnia and Melpomene were metaphors for interpreting life and
art. The word museum, "temple of the muses" is a relic from the Hel-
lenic world. And this temple, the Palm Springs Desert Museum, has its
Mount Olympus called San Jacinto.

Palm Springs Desert Museum

On the TRAIL OF INSPIRATION, we enter the Museum. A ticket taker
with a sense of humor advises to step over to the couple resting on a
bench and to ask them if they have enjoyed themselves. The couple,
really a soft sculpture of two elderly people, is so realistic, I laugh and
wonder why Mom does not.

Familiar with many of the desert creatures shown, I rush through a
darkened room featuring birds, animals and reptiles. Mom lags behind busily using a nifty spotlight button to highlight badger, raccoon,
golden eagle, Cooper's hawk, rabbit and bighorn sheep. Moving along
the displays, learning of the natural history and geology of the
Coachella Valley, we come face to face with the Ice Age mammals that
once roamed the valley floor.

We move through 19th Century Landscapes; featured is Thomas Moran with his large idealized landscapes so instrumental in attracting people to come to the West. After enjoying more Western and Native art, we make a brief visit to the gift shop leaving the art works on the upper level unexplored. On the way out, Mom points out the "stuffed couple" and now laughs. Mom and Dad sit out the rigorous "Muses" trail as I go to challenge my Mount Olympus.

The Museum Trail

The Museum Trail, abruptly rising above Palm Springs, starts directly behind the Museum building. Two descending men, perspiring and red-faced, inquire if I have a picnic lunch to enjoy at the tables on top. This well-marked trail goes straight up for one mile. Aggressive, breath-sapping steep switchbacks propel toward the noonday hot sun. Apollo rides high in the sky.

Finally reaching the junction with the North Lykken Trail and the picnic tables, I welcome the caressing cool breeze. The faint hum of the city rises up. The themes to which the Museum has been dedicated can be vividly visualized on this perch high above the Valley and the ghosts of the past can be brought to life.

The gingersnap-colored, crinkled desert floor stretches out to the gray-blue shape of the mountains beyond, a backdrop to a panorama of the ages. In the mind's eye, enormous ground sloths with bear-like snouts munch on Joshua trees and 450-pound sabre-toothed cats use stabbing teeth to their kill prey. Farther out in the desert, herds of Ice Age mammoths roam the valley floor as they would have 12,000 years ago. This vision disappearing, another appears with the valley underwater. Another mind shift shows Cahuilla natives living as represented in paintings on the Museum walls.

Before descending, I think about the origin of Palm Springs. Ancient Greeks considered wells, springs and fountains, where the sense of connection with the earth was strong, sacred places. Before me is a whole city, Palm Springs, which has sprung up in the sun around bubbling warm water.

Travel notes

The Palm Springs Desert Museum is located in downtown Palm Springs at 101 Museum Drive at Tahquitz Canyon Way, just west of N. Palm Canyon Dr. Open Tuesday through Sunday, closed Mondays and major holidays. Admission fees: adults $12.50, seniors $10.50, students $5.00. Free admission every Thursday from 4-8 p.m., courtesy of the City of Palm Springs. Information: 760-322-4800 or www.psmuseum.org

The strenuous Museum Trail is 1.6 miles round trip, 831 feet elevation change and takes about 1 hour. It is accessed from the corner of the north parking lot.

Greek Muses Tapenade Sandwich

Tapenade:
One 8.75 ounce can Kalamata black olives,
drained and rinsed
2 tablespoons capers, rinsed and drained
2 garlic cloves, minced
1–2 inches anchovy paste
½ cup chunk light tuna in oil, drained
2 tablespoons olive oil
1 teaspoon lemon juice
Pinch cayenne pepper
1 crusty baguette
1 sweet onion, thinly sliced
4 Roma tomatoes, sliced
1 medium cucumber, peeled and sliced into strips lengthwise
½ cup feta or blue cheese, crumbled

· To make tapenade, rinse and pat olives dry. Place in a food processor along with other ingredients. Puree well. Refrigerate overnight.
· Slice baguette into fourths then half horizontally. Generously coat each side of bread with tapenade. Layer sliced vegetables and cheese on one side of bread. Press together two halves of bread. Wrap tightly in plastic wrap and refrigerate until needed. Serves 4.

Trail of Palm Canyon

Aqua Caliente Cultural Museum,
Short hike in Palm Canyon and visit to trading post

&. Spring Cactus Salsa and Prickly Pear Limeade

Baskets on an intriguing poster on a museum door catch the eye telling a story without words about the basket maker, Flora Patencio.
Made from materials rooted in the desert soil, Cahuilla Indian baskets
are intricately woven with designs taken from the natural world: animal tracks, lightening bolts, wind, clouds, birds and creatures of the
land. Native people lived by the elemental powers of nature and everything they fashioned revealed this connection.

Aqua Caliente Cultural Museum

On the TRAIL OF PALM CANYON, Mom and I first enter the Aqua Caliente
Cultural Museum on the Village Green in downtown Palm Springs. A
helpful enthusiastic docent greets and whisks us to view a vintage video
narrated by the famous Cahuilla elder, Katherine Siva Saubel, known
for her achievements in the preservation of Indian languages and culture. Saubel speaks of her childhood with Grandmother, a life when her
people were still hunting and gathering, before the advent of reservation life when they turned to farming and ranching. We gaze into the
eyes of Cahuillas in the old pictures and see pride in their statures and
composure in their faces although the homes in which they lived would
today be considered uninhabitable.

Grandmother cooked in a clay pot over an open fire when they lived in rock caves, cool in summer and warm in winter. An olla, a clay pot, was filled with cooking and drinking water by young girls and carried back to camp. Tasty cakes were made from mesquite bean flour mixed with water and baked in the sun. Camp work was arduous but she remembers her Grandmother always gave thanks to the powers above for the plentiful food.

Though modern inventions like metal buckets could be purchased at the trading post near the original spring in later times, the Cahuilla took pride in making by hand the things needed for daily living. Pottery, introduced into the region only about 1,000 years ago, was hand-shaped from the clay of nearby streams; firing finished the process. We now think of baskets as decorative items but in Grandmother's time some were woven so tightly they held water and could withstand hot rocks placed inside to boil food.

The rare Flora Patencio Basketry Collection in the Museum includes Flora's original tools, natural materials, completed and unfinished baskets. Coiling juncus or sturdy sumac tightly around a deer grass bundle was the common method for making the baskets. Twining, another method for baskets used as strainers, involved the use of whole reeds of juncus or other stems twined into openwork.

In her lifetime spanning nearly a century, 1908–1992, Flora Patencio, the celebrated Cahuilla basket maker of Palm Springs and elder respected for her knowledge of traditional ways, had lived through and adapted to the dramatic forces changing the lives of her people. Quilts, needlework and tatting became her other creative vehicles in later years. But it is in the baskets that I see the weathered face of the maker and feel her hands rough from the many stems she carefully coiled.

The Agua Caliente band of Cahuilla Indians, Flora's people, has lived in the Coachella Valley for two thousand years or more. A parade of passing Spanish and Mexican explorers left the land and people mostly untouched. When the "palm oasis" was found by a U.S. government survey party searching for a southern transcontinental railway route in 1853, things began to change.

Enticement to build rail lines through the desert came from a federal grant in 1876. Ten miles of odd-numbered sections of land adjacent to either side of the tracks went to the Southern Pacific Railroad;

even-numbered sections were for Indian lands. This resulted in the checkerboard pattern so visible on the valley. The same year the U.S. Federal Government deeded in trust to the Agua Caliente people 32,000 acres of which 6,700 are within the city limits of Palm Springs.

Section 14, an Indian holding, is the center of Palm Springs, and as late as the 1920s was where most of the Palm Springs Indians lived in kishes made from palm thatch and wood. The Agua Caliente Tribe is considered to be one of the wealthiest and most influential tribes in the United States. Most all now live in the city. The ancient Indian Canyons, on the National Register of Historic Places, are in the "care of the Tribe," protected for all to visit.

Leaving the preserved remnants of the past inside the Museum with its insight into the day-to-day lives, we proceed by car from the Village Green along South Palm Canyon Drive and pass through the tollgate to the historic Indian Canyons. Here we enter into a land of pristine canyons, a living monument to Cahuilla life and the world's largest stands of fan palms.

Palm Canyon Trail

An ascending road brings us to Hermits Bench. At the bustling Trading Post, Mom and I drop down the steep path to the oases of fan palms.

Listening to our footsteps walking along the Palm Canyon Trail, I am reminded that the Cahuilla have a word describing the pleasant sound. "Gash mo, the sound of the crunching of sand as one walks," is a place name referring to a sandy wash perhaps near where Andreas and Palm Canyon washes flow together. Dictated by the natural world around them, such place names helped the Cahuilla travel skillfully without maps or written language. Young boys learned early the art of walking silently through the snapping dry brush while hunting and the use of landmarks. The challenge to walk noiselessly in the crackling desert becomes too daunting for us as we clomp along.

Mother Nature is not a tidy housekeeper and the fan palm oasis is littered with debris providing welcome shelter for animals and plant nurslings. Over 3,000 native Neowashingtonian filifera, commonly called fan palms, proliferate here with a constant supply of water from year-round streams. The palm was woven into the daily life of the Cahuilla; dwellings were thatched with its leaves, ropes were woven

Palm Canyon Trail, Indian Canyons

with leaf fibers and a few rare baskets stitched with palm fibers. It was a European palmographer who bestowed the name "in honor of the great American."

The world-famous Palm Canyon Trail follows a rippling stream under drowsing palms swaying indolently in the calm air. We proceed down an aisle through their realm calmed by the soft, silken rustle of the fronds. Some well-dressed, clothed in full thatch, others almost denuded and bare, these trees range from tall monarchs to short minions.

If pursued the full 15 miles to its end, Palm Canyon Trail would climb to the Palms-to-Pines Highway 74 in the shadow of the mountain peaks of the Santa Rosas, through a life zone dense with pinyon pines, junipers, red shank and yuccas to a place called Pinyon Flats.

Here, whole Indian families camped and visited while gathering pinyon nuts and hunting game. Travelers used the Palm Canyon Trail heavily to move back and forth from the desert and other parts of Southern California.

Now this long trail is the domain of the hiker and equestrian. Rather than continue we return and a little climb brings us back up to the Trading Post where hanging slivers of rock chime in the wind above Dad resting on a bench. The original trading post, we are informed,

Prickly Pear in bloom

was down in Palm Springs now the site of the Spa Resort Hotel. The tin building of the original Indian Agency, a remnant of the not so glorious past, still stands and can be seen on the way out of the canyon.

Tourists in autos since the 1900s have passed through the same toll gate we exit. Long before that, desert lovers on horseback or on foot traversed the same path to the historic Indian Canyons. Like witnesses in an ancient valley, the silent palms observe all who gather here to heal and nurture on the uneven path.

Travel notes

The Agua Caliente Museum is on the Village Green at 219 South Palm Canyon Drive. Museum hours are Wednesday–Saturday 10 a.m.–5 p.m. and Sunday Noon–5 p.m. Check for summer hours. Information: www.accmuseum.org. Admission is free.

The Indian Canyons are 3 miles south on S. Palm Canyon Drive from the intersection with E. Palm Canyon Drive. Enter the Aqua Caliente Reservation through the tollgate and proceed to the end of the road at the Trading Post. Indian Canyons information: www.indian-canyons.com or 760-323-6018. Open daily October 1-July 4 from 8 a.m. to 5 p.m. and open Friday, Saturday and Sunday July 5-September 30 from 8 a.m. - 5 p.m. Admission fees: adults $9.00, seniors $7, children 6-12 $5, and equestrians $11. This short section of the Palm Canyon trail in this day journey is easy and the stream can be reach in less than a quarter mile. The strenuous Palm Canyon Trail continues on 16 miles one way with an elevation change of 3,566 feet. Smoke Tree Stables information: 760-327-1372.

Spring Cactus Salsa

Nopales is the Mexican name for prickly pear pads. The Cahuilla called them "Navtem." Nopales are readily available in Southern California Mexican markets; also Nopalitos, come in jars, cooked and sliced. Cooked cactus is similar in taste and texture to a dill pickle.

2 cactus paddles, shiny green and unwrinkled
2 boiling onions
2 Roma tomatoes, diced
¼ teaspoon marjoram
½ red onion, minced
½–2 teaspoons finely chopped habanero pepper
(hot) if desired
¼ cup cilantro, chopped
¼ cup olive oil
1 tablespoon lemon juice
¼ teaspoon sea salt
Freshly ground pepper

- Wearing gloves and using a paring knife or vegetable peeler strip bumpy glochids. Trim base and edges of paddle. Slice into 2 by ¼ inch strips.
- Boil cactus and onion in salted water for 15 minutes until tender. Rinse, drain well and cool. Discard onion. Dice cactus strips.
- Shake together olive oil, lemon juice, marjoram, salt and freshly ground pepper.
- Toss with diced cactus, onion, habanero pepper and cilantro. Spoon into pita bread and top with grated white cheese. Serve as salsa with tortilla chips or spoon into inner Romaine lettuce leaves for a salad. Best served fresh. Makes about 1 1/3 cups.

Prickly Pear Limeade

Prickly Pear fruit," Navit tui" was traditionally eaten fresh or dried. We found the light sweet fruit tastes refreshing in a drink.

8 prickly pear fruits
1 cup fresh lime juice
4 tablespoons sugar

- Soak the fruit for 24 hours in water to soften the glochids making them less treacherous to hands. Anchoring with a fork, carefully quarter and scoop out the fruit. Discard peel.
- Mix pulp, lime juice and sugar in blender. Strain out the grape-like seeds. Serve chilled or over ice. Serves 4.

Trail of Murray Canyon

Murray Canyon hike to Seven Sisters Waterfall

ॐ **Summer Raspberry Crisp**

The emerald green of the fan palms and the gold of the sunlit dry foliage interweave to create a rich brocade of landscape on our TRAIL
OF MURRAY CANYON. T.M. and I pass through the Indian tollgate. The
road climbs the alluvial fan and enters a wondrous land of high cliffs
and flowing water at the picnic area of Andreas and Murray Canyons.

Murray Canyon Trail

Murray Canyon, named for the pioneer, Dr. Welwood Murray, features
a 4 mile round trip hike leading to the Seven Sisters, a collection of water
falls. Like the Cahuilla of the old ways, we take shelter in the coolness of
the canyon on this hot day. Sliding under rippling cottonwood trees and
fan palms, we pass through a large picnic area. Set in charred palms, it
appears to be suffering from heavy overuse.

Soon there is a palpable silence as the roar of the Andreas canyon
stream at the parking area becomes a faint murmur. Now between
canyons, out from the shade of the sheltering trees, the brazen sun
blazes down; plants have shriveled and browned to survive the coming
drastic temperatures of a rainless summer. The once perky yellow
flowered brittlebush is now dusty and almost leafless; the remaining
leaves are covered with dense hairs to reflect much of the incoming
sunlight. Occasional thunderstorms could bring back a burst of color.
Not having the adaptability of desert plants and with bodies

Murray Canyon Trail

composed mostly of water, we can only cope by carrying more water and protecting ourselves from the burning noonday sun.

Trails in the Indian canyons, like life, confuse with many choices and junctions. But finding the Murray Canyon trail easy to follow and marked well, we trek the open desert to the first stream crossing. A thorn scratches my leg; the offender the curved talon of a cat claw acacia bush. Sharp-eyed T.M. spots a tiny hummingbird baby resting in a nest of entangling scraggly branches.

A cool stream dominated by fan palms has us winding back and forth on stepping stones. With its height and full array of green and tan fronds, the fan palm imposes and does not reveal that it is actually a giant member of the grass family. These fan palms are sensitive to every caprice of the wind but are seldom downed; the vascular bundling of the base and the bulky trunk provide stability.

A large stone with small round depressions, possibly used for grinding, seems to be the perfect place for lunch. The wind picks up and provides a counter point to the song of palm fronds rustling as if speaking to each other of the intrusion of men and civilization.

Now walking upstream, the canyon narrows and a rock ledge provides cool respite from the stifling heat. After many crisscrosses of the boulder-strewn twisted creek, we reach a horse-tie rack but see no riders. The almost vertical upthrust of rock around us commands respect.

Climbing higher, losing the trail, the timbre of the Seven Sister Falls sings in a different tone from the pitch of the stream and tells us we have scrambled a little too high. Going back down, crossing over the stream, the first spurt of the Falls comes into sight; the hissing and the splashing of water becomes a roar. A gigantic fallen boulder creates a yawning mouth before us.

Dipping bandannas in the cool water, holding them against our necks, we leave the Falls for the return trip. Sadly our packs are now filled with discarded plastic bottles, sad mementos of thoughtless visitors.

Gratefully changing out of hot dusty boots, relaxing under a palapa shelter in the picturesque parking area, the song of the Andreas Canyon stream rings and the rich colors of emerald green palm and golden dried foliage blend for one more unforgettable image of our days in the desert.

Travel notes

The Indian Canyons are 3 miles south on S. Palm Canyon Drive from the intersection with E. Palm Canyon Drive. Enter the Aqua Caliente Reservation through the tollgate and follow the sign to the right to the Andreas/Murray Canyons. Indian Canyons information: www.indian-canyons.com or 760-323-6018. Open daily October 1- July 4 from 8 a.m. to 5 p.m. and open Friday, Saturday and Sunday July 5-September 30 from 8 a.m. - 5 p.m. Admission fees: adults $9.00, seniors $7, children 6-12 $5, and equestrians $11.

This easy 4 mile Murray Canyon hike has 524 feet of elevation change and takes about 2 hours or less. In the spring there may be many water crossings making the trail more moderately strenuous. Smoke Tree Stables information: 760-327-1372

Summer Raspberry Crisp

By late summer Cahuilla were gathering: grass seeds, chia, saltbush seeds, pinyon nuts, palm tree fruit, wild raspberries, blackberries and juniper berries.

4 cups fresh or thawed frozen raspberries
1½ tablespoon lemon juice
⅛ teaspoon nutmeg
⅛ teaspoon cinnamon
1½ cups flour
1½ cups sugar
4 tablespoons butter

- Place raspberries in a greased casserole dish. Spoon lemon juice on berries and sprinkle with nutmeg and cinnamon. Sift together flour and sugar and work in butter until mixture is a crumbly mass. Top berries with mixture.
- Bake at 375 degrees for 1 hour. Serves 8–10.

To make a cup of summer Juniper Tea, crush several juniper berries as a flavor addition to a cup of black tea and sweeten with honey.

Trail of Andreas Canyon

Hike up Andreas Canyon viewing mortars and metates

 Brandied Figs and Mascarpone Cheese

Tahquitz, the evil Cahuilla spirit, is not in a good mood today as we pursue the TRAIL OF ANDREAS CANYON. Mom and Dad see no way to scale the enormous guardian rock before them. Crossing and recrossing a bubbling spring via stones and logs, we are subtly mocked with a chuckling murmur. The secret place ahead will remain unrevealed to them.

Coming to rest on a log, we consider our dilemma and talk about the legend of the Paloverde tree. This legend speaks of the origin of a Paloverde tree at the mouth of the Andreas Canyon. The legendary Tahquitz stole the daughter of the great chief Tachevah. It is said that on the very place where she disappeared into the netherworld, a Paloverde tree sprouted. The daughter, in her new form, the tree, would provide flowers as source of honey, bean pods for cooking and seeds for ground meal for her people. This graceful, small tree with green trunk and widely spreading crown is found extensively in the washes and valleys of the desert.

Mom sees the image of bows of huge ocean-going liners emerging from the rock of the canyon wall before us. Her analogy is not so far fetched. The outcroppings, which Dad guesses to be at least 100 feet high, show evidence of ancient seas.

Andreas Canyon

Andreas Canyon Trail

With a royal-blue dragonfly perched near Mom, I leave them seated next to the offending boulder and move on to find my way in the over-grown jungle of the Andreas Canyon. A woman and five children ahead of me climb like Tarzan up and over the obstructing boulder. They are just like the Cahuilla children in centuries past who would bathe frequently in the cool water on hot summer days.

The trail obscured by many people scrambling, I finally pick it up, wandering alone to the end of the ½ mile path, finding shade under the huge canyon wall and sycamore, cottonwood and palm trees. A chain link fence marks the end of the Indian reservation and the trail. Stone homes in the distance belong to the Andreas Sportsman club.

Making the return trip back down the same side of the stream, I learn the path also crosses over the water and returns down the other side. Ledges jut out. Mom's ocean liners look like stone faces to me with jutting chins, cactus whiskers on prominent jaws reminding that these canyons have drawn many famous human faces to this environment.

Artists, naturalists, photographers and writers were instrumental in publicizing the beauties of the area; many had come for health rea-sons. Carl Eytel, renowned for his pen and ink drawings, used features of the canyons for many of his illustrations. Living under the aegis of the McCallum family, this modest, reserved artist became friend to the Cahuilla, learning their language, customs and songs. Sketching in the canyons, he recorded sun and shadow as seen upon the palms and was known as the "Artist of the Palm." Steve Willard, acclaimed scenic photographer, W.W. Lockwood, the first professional photographer in the area, and Edward Curtis recorded life in these canyons. These men painted a picture of the desert as it was 100 years ago.

A personal hero of mine, John Muir, proponent of the conservation movement in the United States, once camped in Andreas Canyon. With his daughter in ill health, he arrived in the middle of summer at Dr. Welwood Murray's hotel. Finding the heat in town too intense, they moved to a camp in the cool Andreas Canyon.

J. Smeaton Chase, author of Our Araby and other famous guidebooks to the desert, died in 1923. He might be horrified to see the growth on the valley floor today but delighted to see that the canyons remain pristine although they did not become a National Park as he predicted.

The canyon is named for Captain Andreas who farmed at the mouth of the canyon in the last half of the nineteenth century and whose ancestors possibly farmed there before recorded history. Andreas, a resourceful man, built a small adobe house and planted a fig orchard and vineyard.

Near the end of my trail, I pass under the ledges of rock where centuries ago Cahuilla women could have been found grinding mesquite beans, wild oats and acorns in a metate. The summer round of food gathering brought the Cahuilla to the honey mesquite and screwbean trees.

So important was the mesquite, they used its growth stages as one way to partially define and name the seasons of the year: the budding of trees, the blossoming of trees, the forming of beans, the ripening of beans and the falling of beans. Each had its own name and came before the rest of their seasons: midsummer, cool days and cold days. The mesquite meal, possibly ground in the metates I pass, was moistened with water and hardened to form cakes.

When I reappear, Mom and Dad look startled as if I had been gone only a few minutes. That is the magic of Andreas Canyon. Time stands still.

Travel notes

The Indian Canyons are 3 miles south on S. Palm Canyon Drive from the intersection with E. Palm Canyon Drive. Enter the Aqua Caliente Reservation through the tollgate and follow the sign to the right to Andreas/Murray Canyons. Indian Canyons information: www.indian-canyons.com or 760-323-6018. Open daily October 1-July 4 from 8 a.m. to 5 p.m. and open Friday, Saturday and Sunday July 5-September 30 from 8 a.m. - 5 p.m. Admission fees: adults $9.00, seniors $7, children 6-12 $5, and equestrians $11. There are palapas with picnic tables at the parking area.

This easy 2.9 mile Andreas Canyon loop trail has a 442 feet elevation change and takes about 1-1.5 hours. It is a fun hike for kids. Smoke Tree Stables information: 760-327-1372.

Fall Brandied Figs, Pears and Mascarpone Cheese

The Cahuilla grew watermelon, muskmelon, squash, pumpkin, strawberries, figs, peaches, apricots, grapes and pears.

1 cup brandy
⅛ cup sugar
¼ cup figs

· Dissolve sugar in brandy in ceramic bowl. Add figs. Cover and let stand at least 48 hours. Drain. Serve with fresh pears, crusty bread and Mascarpone cheese or cream cheese.

Trail Above City and Tahquitz Falls

Hiking north end of South Lykken Trail viewing
Tahquitz Canyon to Josie Johnson lookout and picnic tables

ë Crunchy Pita Sandwich

In Palm Springs there are streets where the pavement ends and the traveler continues walking up the many uneven footpaths into the mountains. The ability to rise easily above the city, step up and away from its comforts, on paths worn into the soil by trail blazers is unique.

North End of South Lykken Trail

Our TRAIL ABOVE CITY AND TAHQUITZ FALLS finds T.M. and me climbing the north end of the South Lykken Trail, serenaded by chirping birds in the still cool morning air. Feet kick up the familiar trail essence of dust and dried aromatic foliage. In a few hours, the torrid afternoon sun will scorch the abruptly rising unshaded trail. The machines of the city have already begun their assault on the quiet desert. A lone gardener's leaf blower whines like a jet engine. In the distance, a jet takes off riding high into the zenith.

Hiking 35 minutes up the trail, we peer across a wide canyon down a steep escarpment to the rushing water of Tahquitz Canyon Falls. The Falls are dramatic even from this distance. The canyon had been closed for decades to hikers but now is open again.

The oldest Cahuilla village occupied the canyon below, perhaps 2,000 years ago. The canyon is said to have been home to a powerful an-

Ranger-guided hike to Tahquitz Falls

cient shaman, Takwish, in the Indian language. This supernatural being from the Cahuilla creation time lived here and in all these mountains.

The Cahuilla women dressed in grass skirts and the men in loin cloths wearing sandals of yucca and agave would not have looked the part of the stereotypical Indian of the Plains with headdress and beaded buckskins. The climate did not call for such elaborate clothing. Robes of rabbit skin warmed in winter and buckskin boot-like shoes protected feet on mountain trails.

The familiar buffalo-skin teepee of Western paintings had no place in this village. A home was a kish, a circular brush shelter built over a hollow in the ground with a roof thatched with tules or other plants. To the Indians "a house was not forever" and they moved frequently.

Plentiful water, plants and animals made for a good life; melons, squash, beans and corn grew easily. Plants and seeds were gathered for food, medicines and basket weaving. In the early twentieth century, one could still find Cahuilla children bathing and splashing in the cool water under the waterfall.

Wishing for the cool of the flowing waters, we turn our attention back to the dusty trail. A climb of 1,000 vertical feet in 50 minutes brings us to the Josie Johnson Vista Park. A tie rack for horses stands empty. A quail cries plaintively. A wooden cross with the name Hoffman stands guard on this hazy day in May.

The South Lykken Trail does continue to its south end but we are content to end our journey here. Hurried footsteps with waning strength bring one quickly down to permanent roads and civilization.

Travel notes

The north end of the South Lykken Trail starts at the west end of Mesquite Road off South Palm Canyon Drive. There are picnic tables at both north and south ends. The moderate South Lykken trail hike from the north end to the Josie Johnson lookout and return is 2.8 miles, 1000 foot elevation change and takes about 1.5-2 hours.

The Tahquitz Canyon hike to a spectacular 60-foot waterfall starts at the visitor center at 500 West Mesquite, off South Palm Canyon Drive. The Tahquitz Canyon visitor center is open daily October- July for self–guided hikes from 7:30 am -5 p.m. July-September it is open only Friday, Saturday and Sunday. Ranger-led interpretive hikes depart from the visitor center at 8 am, 10 am, noon, and 2 p.m. Admission: $12.50 adults and $6 children 12 and under. Reservations and information: www.tahquitzcanyon.com or 760-416-7044

The easy to moderate Tahquitz loop is 2 miles roundtrip and has an elevation change of 350 feet and will take about 1.5 to 2.5 hours. Hikers need to be in reasonably good shape.

Crunchy Pita Sandwich

1 can 6½ oz water packed tuna, drained
½ cup shredded carrots
½ cup chopped celery
¼ cup green onion, chopped with some green stem
½ cup mayonnaise
¼ cup green olives, chopped
1 can shoestring potatoes
Pita bread

· Combine all ingredients except pita and shoestring potatoes. Cover and chill. For the trail, spoon into pita bread and seal in sandwich bag. Bring potatoes separately to sprinkle on top. Serves 4.

Trail of John G. McCallum

*Visit to McCallum Adobe/Historical Society
and Cornelia White Home on the Village Green*

&❧ Scottish Shortbread

If the name John Guthrie McCallum does not ring a bell in Western history like a Wyatt or Virgil Earp who grew up in nearby San Bernardino maybe it is because this significant figure in the Far West was unquestionably one of the good guys in white hats. But let's start with the everyday world of John G. McCallum in the modest adobe McCallum home.

McCallum Adobe

Situated on the Village Green, a historic preserve of four buildings set in a small circular oasis on Palm Canyon Drive, it has been moved from its original location where it was built in the 1880s, at the southwest corner of Palm Canyon Drive and Tahquitz Canyon Way, to where it now stands on the Green. On our TRAIL OF JOHN G. MCCALLUM, we pass an olla vase fountain playing pleasing water melodies and enter the dark interior of the oldest remaining structure in Palm Springs. Here we learn the story and glimpse the life of John G. McCallum.

At fifty-seven years, this son of a Scottish farmer was a handsome man with a wife, five children and impressive credentials as a respected San Francisco attorney, politician and editor. McCallum's call to the adventure of the desert was not for personal glory or greed for gold; his beloved child Johnny was afflicted with life-ravaging tuberculosis.

While McCallum worked as an Indian agent to the Mission Indians in San Bernardino, friend and Banning Indian guide, Will Pablo, led him to a sleepy reservation village near the base of the San Jacinto mountains where hot water bubbled out of the ground. In tiny Aqua Caliente, McCallum saw hope for Johnny's health in the ancient Indian traditions of using healing mineral waters; the positive effect of the desert air was also welcome.

His family moved into a rough camp near a gray-trunked old fig tree in a valley, which they named Palm. No white settler was ever known to have lived there permanently. No longer an Indian agent, he came only as an advocate and friend to the Cahuilla people.

Members of the tribe were employed by him to make bricks in an ancient way by mixing earth and water. These adobe bricks, moved from the original home, surround us now. Indians also helped him "bring water to the land," as they had done in the past; construction of a 19-mile stone-lined aqueduct from the Whitewater River tapped the water of the snows of Mount San Gorgonio. A variety of crops were tested to see what irrigation could help grow in the desert. McCallum grew oranges, grapes and apricots. He also promoted the growing of fruit in the area. Eventually, along with three other men, he founded the Palm Valley Land and Water Company.

Acquiring land in various parcels, his holdings increased to 1,767 acres; these included the 320 acres that would eventually comprise the heart of downtown Palm Springs where we walk.

His work that began in 1884 was the ripple that became an ever-widening story revealed to us as we trace the history trail of Palm Springs through the Historical Society presentations located inside the Adobe. A short video shows a colorful array of citizens who took a sleepy village on a narrow road along the base of the mountains to an international destination city, known today for renewal of the body and spirit. Surprising to us are the many pioneer women honored along with the men. They influenced the growth and development by imparting their own values and dreams.

A striking black and white photograph on the wall brings to life a clutch of ladies picnicking in Palm Canyon with distinguished-looking Dr. Welwood Murray. The leg-o-mutton sleeves on the long dresses they wear show turn-of-the-century fashion. A simple picnic lunch of which only the apples remain and a large graniteware coffee pot set directly onto coals completes an intriguing picture.

Dr. Welwood Murray of the photograph, whose title, Doctor, came during the Civil War, built the first hotel in town in 1887. Seeing the healing virtue of hot curative water, he built a bathhouse directly over hot springs leased from the Indians. About the size of a modern hot tub, mud covered the bottom. Today, the Spa Hotel and Casino occupies the land of the original spring. It may be seen preserved on the grounds.

The entrepreneurs Murray and McCallum successful in their own endeavors began a campaign to promote the desert. Flyers distributed to San Francisco, Los Angeles and Riverside advertised an excursion to Palm Springs:

> *The greatest summer resort in the world.*
> *Home of the banana, date and orange.*
> *No fog! no frost! no wind storms!*
> *Auction November 1, 1887.*

The people attracted by the ad left on the train from San Francisco for a $25 fare and traveled through Los Angeles. At Seven Palms, a greeter in flowing Arabian robes with camel in tow met them. After being entertained with music, they were put into carriages and driven through the forbidding desert to Murray's Hotel, considered a "lovely oasis fairyland." Succumbing to the "romance of the desert," visitors bid against each other and $50,000 worth of land was sold. The settlement was established and things prospered for the McCallum family. But the desert is not a place with which to trifle.

In 1890, many pioneer farmers started to lose their crops. Some landowners stopped paying their share of the water levy for the Tahquitz aqueduct. But the worst was yet to come for John McCallum. In 1891, Johnny died at the young age of twenty-six years. A father's hope and a family's sacrifice was not enough to save a life.

Another test of the Palm Valley colonists and McCallum's grit came in the form of a 21 day rainfall followed by an 11 year drought which began in 1894. The deluge and lack of rain drove most all the new settlers except McCallum and Murray out of the valley. Another son of John McCallum, Wallace, died in 1896. The following year McCallum, one must think brokenhearted, died. Even after his death, tragedy for his family continued.

The McCallum clan was struck another blow when last son Harry died, also of tuberculosis, and their interest in the Palm Valley Water Co. was sold because of financial hardship. Pearl, the favored youngest daughter, and her mother returned to their desert home and picked up the reins. By 1905, the rains returned and so did visitors and residents. The pictures we have seen in the historic house have allowed us to share the life of John McCallum vicariously. Intrigued, we plan to follow the adventures of daughter Pearl.

We emerge from the cool Adobe to find Dad waiting patiently on the bench outside. Engrossed, we had told him 15 minutes at the most but we have spent almost 2 hours going back in time. Out in the present day for a moment, we reenter the past through another door; this one of a home constructed with used railroad ties.

Cornelia White Home

The little Cornelia White home, also a low ranch-style with shake roof and stone fireplace, next to the McCallum Adobe has been moved and moved again since Welwood Murray built it in 1893. The wood used in its construction was recycled from a defunct narrow gauge railroad, as it was a valuable commodity in those times.

Dr. Welwood Murray, struggling to hang on through the low times having lost many of his fruit trees, tried but failed in 1908 to sell his hotel to a guest and soon to be a younger new force in town, Nellie Coffman. Dr. Murray died in 1914. His hotel and the rest of the block to the south was bought by Dr. Florilla White and her sister Miss Cornelia White, also soon to be influential and popular women of Palm Springs.

Antiques in the home, donated by local residents, complete a picture of life of the pioneer era in Palm Springs. When the White sisters came to town in 1914, Palm Springs was only two blocks long with no electricity or telephones. Coal oil lamps and candles illuminated homes where cooking was done on coal or wood-burning stoves. Jean, the docent, makes life in this house and its era come alive especially for Mom who also grew up with a grandmother who cooked on a black iron wood burning stove with isinglass windows. She remembers the pokers used to lift the round lids on top of the stove to feed the fire. In Jean's opinion a pie crust was never as good as one cooked by her Palm Springs pioneer family on an old-fashioned range.

As we leave the little house, the sun sets over Palm Springs as it did for these pioneers whose lives so vividly exist in our minds now. John G. McCallum, a good guy, left a legacy for his daughter, Pearl, of grit, determination and a love for the desert that would continue the saga of the McCallum family well into the twentieth century.

Travel notes

The McCallum Adobe on the Village Green is at 221 South Palm Canyon Drive. Hours: Wednesday and Sunday, Noon–3 p.m. and Thursday through Saturday, 10 a.m.–4 p.m. Check for summer hours: 760-323-8297. Admission fee: nominal. The Spa Hotel and Casino and the original spring is at 100 North Indian Canyon Drive.

Scottish Shortbread

1 cup butter
½ cup powdered sugar
2 cups all-purpose flour
¼ teaspoon salt
¼ teaspoon baking powder

- Work room temperature butter with spoon until creamy. Add sugar gradually working until light.
- Stir baking powder and salt into flour. Add dry ingredients to butter mixture gradually. When ball forms knead 10 times with hands. Chill until easy to handle. Pat dough evenly into 2 ungreased 9 inch round cake pans. Mark each pan into 8 triangles with a fork pricking through dough.
- Bake at 350 degrees Fahrenheit for 15 minutes until delicately browned. Cool and cut along marked sections. Makes 16 shortbreads. Can be frozen.

Trail of Pearl and Nellie, Two Women of Vision

Downtown Walking Tour: Oasis Tower, McCallum Adobe, Tennis Club, Thomas O'Donnell House and George Roberson House (Le Vallauris)

ह**•** Short Ration Cake

Pay the taxes ... hold onto the land.

These wise words of John G. McCallum became a mantra to his daughter Pearl after his death in 1897. One by one, the three McCallum brothers had succumbed to the scourge of the times, tuberculosis, and other disease. The death of her brother Harry, who had been running the Palm Valley ranch, brought Pearl and her mother back to the McCallum adobe home. The health of her mother and her own studies had kept her away in Los Angeles until this time. This call back to her beloved desert was in difficult economic circumstances; they were forced to sell their interest in the Palm Valley Water Company.

Pearl found a village far different from her childhood and it seemed that her pioneer father's name had been almost forgotten. Determined that his legacy not be lost, she embarked upon a lifetime of business and philanthropic adventures.

Her marriage in 1914 to Austin G. McManus, a real estate magnate, was another strong guiding influence for our heroine. Consequently becoming a skilled, sharp land dealer, offering for sale many parcels of the land held by her father, the frugal Scot discovered methods to hold on to what was destined to develop into the immensely valuable Palm

Downtown Palm Springs
Photo credit: Palm Springs Bureau of Tourism

Canyon Drive frontage we walk. The sale of her properties and the development of projects such as the first apartment building in town, the Oasis Hotel and the Tennis Club, made her a major financial player in the city. Her generosity included donating land, setting up scholarship programs and underwriting numerous charities.

World War II brought General Patton and his men to the desert in 1942 preparing for their test of fire in Africa against Vichy French and German forces. Shrewdly, Mrs. Pearl McManus bought more land at this time, foreseeing that the soldiers would come back after the war. And they did in great numbers.

Our TRAIL OF PEARL AND NELLIE is not along the uneven paths of the young Pearl's village but the smooth palm-studded streets of a world-renowned city where her influence can still be seen.

Oasis Tower

In 1924, Austin and Pearl selected Lloyd Wright, the young son of Frank Lloyd Wright, to design the Moderne/Art Deco Oasis Hotel as a tribute to her father, John G. McCallum.

We are able to find the only remaining original part of this historic hotel at 121 South Palm Canyon Drive, set behind commercial buildings on Palm Canyon Drive. The Art Deco style is to be seen in this singular 40-foot tower that accessed the roof top terrace and upper rooms, one of which was said to have been a favorite of Loretta Young, a very popular movie star of the day. The current operating Oasis Hotel, which includes the tower, is entered off Tahquitz Canyon Way around the corner.

McCallum Adobe on the Village Green

Walking further south on Palm Canyon Drive, we find another significant preserved part of the McCallum history set on the Village Green. After the land under the original McCallum family home was sold by Mrs. McManus, she donated this Palm Canyon Drive frontage at 221 South Palm Canyon Drive, with the stipulation that the adobe home be preserved there.

Inside, we are welcomed by Sally Hall McManus of the pioneer family McManus. Kindly responding to our newcomer questions, she suggests books that are available from the Historical Society. Her desk piled with new acquisitions for the Historical Society, she fields questions from a couple hoping their home has starlet history.

From here our itinerary takes us strolling a scant block south on Palm Canyon Drive and we turn right on Baristo Road following it to its west end where the mountain meets the desert. One hundred years ago, we would have walked among fig, orange and apricot trees into John McCallum's grape arbors and looked out upon alfalfa fields in his agricultural vision for the village. Instead, we find the prestigious Tennis Club nestled under the mountain, another landmark on our Trail.

The Tennis Club

Observing the popularity of tennis on trips to Europe, Mrs. McManus was inspired to build the first tennis courts in town and they were considered to be some of the best in the world.

We find the courts and pools humming with activity. In fact, we are informed proudly the private club had just celebrated its sixtieth year anniversary. In 1937 the Tennis Club was the "in" place for the Palm

Springs high society and Mrs. McManus socialized with the many celebrities and business tycoons around the grounds and pool.

Her struggle to establish herself in Palm Springs and to fulfill her goal of indelibly stamping her father's name, John G. McCallum, upon Palm Springs along with her strong will, is said to have brought her into contention with many parties. But in later years hard feelings softened as she continued with her benevolent work. Financial support for many projects included the McCallum Desert Foundation that has awarded over 4 million dollars in grants even after her death in 1966. The many beneficiaries of this largess are spread widely throughout the city. Her works support high schools, colleges, hospitals, museums, nature centers and the list goes on and on, touching almost every corner of the Coachella Valley.

Now at the end of our Trail of the visionary daughter of the first pioneer founding family of Palm Springs, we remember her best by the Historical Society portrait showing her with serious demeanor astride a beautiful horse at the age of 80, a trim athletic woman with short cropped hair, in western dress posed confidently in the desert with the magnificent mountains she and her father so loved in the background.

Nellie Coffman, the Mother of Palm Springs

Another Historical Society portrait introduces us to the "Mother of Palm Springs. " Our Trail of another visionary woman of the desert begins. Nellie Coffman, said to have been a rival of Pearl, influenced the city in her own inimitable way. This outstanding woman foresaw a future need for Los Angeles city dwellers to find sanctuary in the desert on her very first visit to the dusty little village.

Said to have arrived unannounced in a sand storm, Nellie and her husband Dr. Harry Coffman, received an unceremonious welcome at Dr. Welwood Murray's Palm Springs hotel, the only hotel in town. They were permitted to stay only by agreeing to wash their dishes after meager fare of tea, toast, oatmeal and prunes. However, the beauty of the desert immediately overcame the obstacles of their stay and finding the dry desert air healthful, they soon became permanent residents. Thus began the adventures of another prominent female heroine of the city who came to be called affectionately, Mother Coffman.

In 1909, purchasing a bungalow on two acres, Nellie and her husband turned it into a boarding house and sanitorium catering to guests with asthma and arthritis. Tent houses made of canvas and wood were added for the burgeoning number of guests. Life-threatening tuberculosis brought many "lungers" to the sanitorium. Many who came to the desert for their health were artists, authors, naturalists and photographers who in time communicated to the world the breathtaking landscape of this desert.

But by 1915, Nellie's vision that Palm Springs would be a playground for more than just the infirm caused her to begin excluding guests with communicable diseases from the hotel. "No invalids," became a policy.

The 1920s discovery of a large underground pool of water, ironically below the forbidding surface of the desert, brought about tremendous change. With the main obstacle to growth in the desert overcome, booming Palm Springs attracted Hollywood celebrities from the new film making industry in Los Angeles. Sanitoriums became hotels and guests began to flock to the Desert Inn run by Mother Coffman.

The conflagration of World War I caused the European rich and famous to look for a new playground. They found it at Nellie's door at the Desert Inn, now a complex of luxurious Spanish-style guesthouses set in a 35-acre garden. Her dream of a sanctuary for city dwellers became a haven for the worldwide war-weary.

Described as a tenacious pioneer, she operated the hotel with her two sons, George and Earl, for more than 40 years. When World War II erupted Nellie and her hotel were thrust into national prominence once again. Palm Springs was considered a haven behind the barrier of mountains, safe from a possible Japanese attack on the coast. Mother Coffman posted humorous signs in guest rooms containing poems like this about the war shortages affecting the hotels:

> *Sherman was right. War is hell.*
> *Please don't scold the maid, she's not to blame-*
> *You're short on towels, and that's a shame.*
> *But Uncle Sammy, brave and wise,*
> *has asked us to economize.*
> *If this restriction leaves you numb,*
> *Wait'll we tackle sugar, chum.*

On foot, we search for visible remnants of this pioneer woman who shaped the hospitality of Palm Springs. We walk Tahquitz Canyon Way toward the mountains from the corner of Palm Canyon Drive looking for the place where once the world's elite gathered at the subdued, elegant Desert Inn.

Nellie Coffman's Desert Inn

Gone is the "splendid palm lined horseshoe drive flanked by expensive glittering cars," at the main entrance to the Desert Inn on Palm Canyon Drive and Tahquitz Canyon Way. Silent is the laughter of capricious guests enjoying lunch on the paved front patio or along the wide porch and there is no splashing of the who's who of Hollywood in the first swimming pool in Palm Springs. Although this dynamic woman thought her hotel, would still stand well into the twentieth century, one of the most prestigious hotels in the city's history has disappeared.

When Nellie died peacefully in her eighties, 41years after the purchase of her first boarding house, business in Palm Springs came to a stand still. A simple graveside tribute at the exclusive Welwood Murray pioneer cemetery marked the passing of an era and a great lady.

The Desert Inn was sold in 1955 and in 1967 the land was developed for what is now a shopping mall, the Desert Fashion Plaza. In 1976, the Palm Springs Desert Museum took its place on the former rear grounds of the hotel.

Walking on Tahquitz Canyon Drive, we pass the Desert Fashion Plaza and the Desert Museum. Surely there must be some remnant of Nellie's hotel for us to see.

Thomas O'Donnell Home

Our eyes rise above the Museum to a home set high above the desert floor. It is a Mediterranean Revival-style home with red-tiled gable roof featuring an encircling porch. Visible from most points in the city, this house built in 1925 by Nellie Coffman for Thomas O'Donnell was an architectural match to her Desert Inn.

George Roberson House, Le Vallauris Restaurant

Now leaving the Desert Fashion Plaza area, we walk farther west on Tahquitz Canyon Way. Another Coffman landmark comes into view.

It is a Mediterranean Spanish Revival home at 385 West Tahquitz Canyon Way built by Nellie Coffman's son George Roberson. The home shaded by trees, is now a five-star restaurant called Le Vallauris.

Anxious to see the interior, we are graciously welcomed by staff and seated outside on the patio fragrant with flowers. After a delicious lunch of Lake Superior whitefish, we read about the past guests to the restaurant. Never star-struck or impressed by pretension, Nellie still would probably be proud to know that Le Vallauris diners have included President and Mrs. Gerald Ford, the Frank Sinatras, the Bob Hopes and many others.

Just as the portrait of Pearl McCallum gave us insight into the woman she was, the pictures of Nellie Coffman reveal to us an ample motherly figure quite capable of enfolding the whole world in her arms.

No trail of the desert would be complete without tracing the footsteps and lives of these two women born in the late 1800s endowed with strong wills and ingenuity. The extraordinary Colorado Desert has drawn people of extraordinary vision. We, the future people Pearl and Nellie foresaw as needing respite, find ourselves a bit nostalgic for the days of their tiny village.

Travel notes

The McCallum Adobe on the Village Green is at 221 South Palm Canyon Drive. Hours: Wednesday and Sunday: Noon–3 p.m. Thursday through Saturday, 10 a.m.–4 p.m. Check for summer hours: 760-323-8297. Small admission fee, no charge for children with adult.

The tower of the Oasis Hotel, set behind the commercial buildings, can be seen from 121 South Palm Canyon Drive. The private Tennis Club is at the west end of Baristo Road. La Vallauris Restaurant, the former George Roberson home, is at 385 West Tahquitz Canyon Way. Information: 760-325-5059.

Short Ration Cake

1 cup brown sugar firmly packed
1¼ cup water
1/3 cup vegetable shortening
2/3 cup raisins
¼ teaspoon nutmeg
2 teaspoons cinnamon
¼ teaspoon ground cloves
½ teaspoon salt
1 teaspoon baking soda
2 teaspoons water
2 cups all purpose flour
1 teaspoon baking powder

- Boil brown sugar, 1¼ cup water, shortening, raisins and spices together for 3 minutes. Cool. Dissolve salt and baking soda in 2 teaspoons water and add to sugar mixture. Stir together baking powder and flour and add gradually, beating smooth after each addition. Bake in greased and floured 8x8x2 pan at 325 degrees Fahrenheit about 45 minutes or until toothpick comes out clean.

Trail of Carl Lykken

Challenging hike up North Lykken Trail then descending to downtown Palm Springs via Museum Trail

ॐ Stuffed Pickles

Communication was Carl Lykken's business. When you ran the post office, had the only telephone in town and a telegraph service, you were a pretty popular guy, especially if you also ran a general merchandise emporium. Carl Lykken first hung out his sign in 1914 on Palm Canyon Drive.

J. Smeaton Chase in his guidebook to the 1920s Palm Springs stated: "rural free delivery does not entice us; we prefer the daily gathering at the store at mail time, Indians and whites together where we can count on catching Miguel or Romualda if we wish to hire a pony or get the washing done." That pretty much sets the mood of the inhabitants at that time.

North Lykken Trail

On the TRAIL OF CARL LYKKEN, pioneer and early settler, we step up from the heart of the city. The trail named in honor of the founding member of the Desert Riders splits immediately and we take the less strenuous path to the right. This trail, mostly up outcropping rock, is like a rocky staircase. Rapidly we climb high above Palm Springs, which now looks like a Lego Set city. The checkerboard Coachella Valley sprawls from Desert Hot Springs in the north and the eye follows the antelope-tan Little San Bernardino Mountains with sand hills in

Palm Springs from Carl Lykken Trail

the foreground, down to hazy, distant Palm Desert. At this height, the Bob Hope house is a silvery rectangle beyond the entrance to Palm Canyon. Blue swimming pools sparkle in whimsical shapes outside miniature mansions below.

The noise of the city drifts up as leaf blowers and saws drone. The ping-pong of bouncing balls echoes from the tennis courts below. Palm Springs pioneer, Pearl McCallum McManus, built the prestigious Tennis Club.

The trail meanders. We lose it several times. Dad threatens to go back. Mom says, "You're getting puny." We leave them laughing on the desert-varnished rocks photographing Dad against a steep escarpment hoping to capture the power of the earth forces and the delicate flowering brittlebush. Mom remarks that this trail should only be recommended for mountain goats and more agile people. However, a line of spry senior citizens, mountain goats, is streaming up the popular trail behind us.

T.M. and I pause to look down to distant Palm Canyon Drive where Carl Lykken's store once stood. Soon the North Lykken intersects the Skyline Trail. Near the junction of the two trails a scrawled sign says: "8 miles to Round Valley Ranger station, 10 hour hike and no water." Back in the days when the Tram did not exist, this difficult route brought travelers to the top of San Jacinto.

Above us on this trail we see a hiker, a semi-nude hiker, on his way toward us—surely he has seen us and will—OOPS—he makes the turn and comes face to face with us. His rolled-down white briefs just cover his private parts. We laugh—he could not be a true nudist; his buns are too lily white.

After an hour of hiking, we reach the picnic tables above the Palm Spring Desert Museum and junction with the Museum Trail. We leave the North Lykken Trail that continues north and drop down to town on the Museum Trail finishing in just under two hours. Stepping off the dusty mountain trail onto the streets of downtown, we join the casual strollers who gather daily just like those walkers of past days but now meet at coffee houses and restaurants along the palm-studded avenue.

Travel notes

The North Lykken trailhead is at the west end of Ramon Road in downtown Palm Springs. This day journey described is a moderate 2 mile section of the North Lykken Trail combined with a 1 mile descent down the Museum Trail for a total of 3 miles. It will take about 2 hours plus about 30 minutes to walk back through town to the end of Ramon Road where the hike began.

At the beginning of the Trail, the left fork seems easier to follow. The Trail to the right meanders making it easy to get confused but it does have more views of the city.

Stuffed Dill Pickle

In Wonders of the Colorado Desert, George Wharton James described the Palm Valley store as a "typical desert place, where the prospector and traveler, the tent-dweller and the hunter, may alike replenish his stock of canned and other eatables and procure feed for his animals." They probably also dipped into the pickle and cracker barrels.

· Drain and blot large old-fashioned dill pickle. Hollow out and stuff with deviled ham, tuna salad or slivers of Pecorino Romano cheese. Wrap tightly in food wrap. Refrigerate. For the trail, take several hard-boiled eggs.

· Another old-fashioned picnic sandwich idea that came to us through English and Scottish relatives is a "fold-over." Using a loaf of soft white bread simply make sandwiches by spreading one slice bread with jam or jelly and "folding over." A "piece" is a folded over sandwich with meat.

Trail of a Self-Directed Spa Day

*Hike South Lykken Trail to Simonetta Kennett Vista Point
and visit to Welwood Murray Memorial Library*

&▲ Spa Fruit Salad and Orange, Ginger and Raisin Scone

Sunrise hikers from a nearby posh hotel, having already crisscrossed
the rugged slopes of the San Jacinto Mountains under the direction
of a fitness advisor, file past us out of the wash. Dad comments, "I can't
believe so many people enjoy torturing themselves." Our curmudgeon
of hiking, merely getting his short jaunt "over with," hasn't gotten into
the "spa aspect" of hiking yet.

South Lykken Trail

On our TRAIL OF A SELF-DIRECTED SPA DAY, we begin on South Palm
Canyon Drive following a dike to the trailhead. At 9:30 a.m. every rock
and bush is exposed starkly in the blazing sun. The early morning people could have found the purple mountains awash in pinks and blues.
Now the shadows are driven back to lurk, wait and to return when the
daystar has fallen once more.

Walking along, Mom and I ponder as to why a hike in the desert
can be comparable to a day at a spa. Soon such thoughts are forgotten
as the spectacle of the San Jacinto Mountains and adjoining valleys
rolls out.

When the elevation starts to rise at the trailhead, Dad, hip trou-
bling, decides his walk is over and retreats to an unfinished crossword
puzzle in the car. Soon after I lose Mom, afraid of slipping and falling

Author's parents on the South Lykken Trail

on the trail. Nagging, I tell her to shed her city shoes and get into some sensible hiking boots.

I leave her happily perched on a rock overshadowed by a brown upthrust of boulder. Rocks here are the relics of a time long ago when cataclysmic forces were at work on the planet. Armed with pen, paper and botanical guidebook, she relaxes, identifying surrounding plants like the red barrel cactus. She will wait, bravely sharing her rock with a tiny skink. My hike will be one hour total, out and back. Not quite out of earshot I hear, " Do you think there could be rattle snakes?" Laughing, I think for once she probably has reason to worry but not at this time of the day.

She quickly becomes a miniature figure sitting in a bowl of silence looking down upon an ancient wash dotted with creosote bush respectfully distanced one from the other as detailed by nature's water rights. Scientists believe a kind of chemical warfare spaces desert plants.

I am ushered along the trail by the ubiquitous brittlebush, mounded hemispheres of perky yellow blossoms on gray-green crowns, set like jewels in a woman's ring. Boulders painted with lime-colored lichen are strewn in the wash below amid silvery sage chaparral. A short distance up the trail, a high country vista and silence are a welcome reward. All to be heard are the sloshing of a water bottle swinging from my fanny pack and the rhythmic tapping of my wooden walking stick. The bright blue sky is broken only by slashes of white jet air trails.

Simonetta Kennett Vista Point

Twenty-five minutes of hiking brings me to the Simonetta Kennett Vista Point and picnic tables for the south side of the Lykken Trail. Once more the view expands, this time taking in the city. Two black crows cawing and a Cooper's hawk riding on invisible thermals circle above. Rain dissolved, windblown particles have darkened and "desert varnished" the surrounding rock surfaces. The trail goes on but it is time to turn back.

Taking one long last look, I am reminded of something Mom had read about Charles Dickens; the names of his characters fit exactly, revealing their personalities. The names Tiny Tim and Scrooge immediately evoke an image. The San Jacinto massif is aptly named and reveals its personality in jutting jagged peaks. The nearby Santa Rosas, also like their name, are softer, more eroded.

Back at the wash, Mom's knowledge of the creosote bush now includes the medicinal qualities of it. The Cahuilla Indians considered it to be their medicine chest; but not versed in their skills, we will have to resort to the drugstore.

A small tree, like a puff of smoke in the desert wash, edges our way back down the well-worn path. The smoke tree's dense fine hairs pressed against the stem color it a silver gray. The desert air is like an aromatic herb inhalant in a spa.

Finished with our exercise portion of the spa day and wanting to exercise our minds as well, we arrive at the car. Hot and happy to see us, Dad heads downtown to the busy corner of South Palm Canyon and Tahquitz Canyon Drives where we find the Welwood Murray Memorial Library.

Welwood Murray Memorial Library

In 1938 George Welwood Murray donated the land on which the library building stands as a memorial to his pioneer father, Dr. Welwood Murray, with the understanding that a library would be built on the site by the newly incorporated city of Palm Springs. Opening in February of 1941, it was a branch of the city library until 1992 but now seems more like an information booth for downtown strollers.

"Everyone out! It's 1 o'clock."

Is this last call at the local bar? No, just the efficient and prompt summer afternoon closing of the library. Rushing past pictures of Palm Springs with cars of the 1930s and the day it snowed downtown, we long to linger over other nostalgic pictures but we have come too late.

Just before the witching hour, we look up the meaning of a word in Webster's Dictionary about which we have had a slight disagreement. The word "escarpment" is found to be, "an abrupt face of a high ridge." Satisfied, both are a little right about the escarpment between the San Jacinto Mountains and the adjacent Coachella Valley as one of the boldest in North America.

The clock strikes 1:00 p.m. and we are out on the street.

Seated at a sidewalk café, quietly reflecting upon our spa day, the taste of the desert lingers like a fine dry wine. The therapeutic value of a day in the desert is indisputable whether taken in a spa setting or in our more casual way with only the cost of tired legs. Even our curmudgeon of hiking agrees. A short walk up the wash, observing from a rock or climbing all the way to the top brings spiritual and physical rewards. The real glory of the land belongs to those adventurous enough to just go.

Travel notes

The South Lykken Trail has a trailhead on both north and south ends. The north end starts at the parking lot at the west end of Mesquite Road and South Palm Canyon Drive. The south end (where this hike starts) is on South Palm Canyon Drive just past the intersection of Murray Canyon Drive and Palm Canyon Drive. Follow the dike to the trailhead. Picnic tables are located at both north and south ends of the trail. The entire strenuous South Lykken Trail is 4.4 miles one way with a 1004 foot elevation change. But this moderate day journey hike to the Vista Point is about 2 miles and will take about 1 hour.

The Welwood Murray Library is closed at the time of this writing. It is scheduled to reopen as a branch of the Palm Springs Library.

Spa Fruit Salad

1 cup firm strawberries, halved
1 cup green or red seedless grapes, halved
4 kiwis, peeled and sliced
1 cup cantaloupe, peeled, seeded and diced
1 cup honeydew melon, peeled, seeded and diced
½ cup honey
Juice of ½ orange
Juice of ½ lime
1 teaspoon poppy seeds

- Stir juices into honey. Add poppy seeds. Toss dressing with fruit. Refrigerate. Serves 4.

Orange, Ginger and Raisin Scones

2 cups flour
1/3 cup sugar
½ teaspoon each baking soda and salt
2 teaspoons baking powder
5 tablespoons cold butter
1 egg, beaten
2/3 cup low fat buttermilk
½ cup raisins
1 tablespoon zest of orange
1 tablespoon crystallized ginger, finely chopped

- Preheat oven to 400 degrees. Stir together in chilled bowl flour, sugar, baking soda, baking powder and salt. Cut cold butter into pieces and rub into dry ingredients using fingers until butter is broken up and coarse crumbs form.
- Stir in beaten egg and buttermilk to make a soft dough. Mix in raisins, ginger and orange zest.

- Place dough on lightly floured board and knead 5 to 7 times. Separate dough in half and make circles about 6 inches in diameter and ½–¾ inch thick. Cut each circle into six wedges.
- Place scones on greased baking sheet leaving space between. Bake about 15–20 minutes until tops are golden brown and puffy. If desired sprinkle with a mixture of sugar and cinnamon. Cool on rack. Can be frozen and reheated in the oven. Makes 12.

Trail of the Pony Express

*Hiking Garstin Trail rising to a plateau
connecting with Berns and Araby trails*

⊱ Pony Express Quick Black Bean and Tuna Pan Bagna

Weekly, a subsidiary of the Pony Express pursued the state of the art in fast communication between Yuma, Arizona and San Bernardino, California. Grabbing the mochilla, mounting a fresh mustang, tearing along the Indian trails on the way to Aqua Caliente, the Pony Express Rider flew. The tragedy of one intrepid rider in Hawk Canyon brought to a close this local colorful phenomenon of the West.

Garstin Trail

On our TRAIL OF THE PONY EXPRESS in the Coachella Valley, we are off like a shot up the Garstin Trail on our way to the plateau of Smoke Tree Mountain.

Our jump-start ends as the steep switchback rise of the Garstin Trail gives Mom and Dad some difficulty. A quarter-mile up the trail, a rock set against the mountain becomes her seat to savor the 180-degree view and he stands by patiently. Picking up rocks with striations of rusty-red and gray intermingled and some gray-white rock, she discovers the color of the distant gentle giants of mountains.

A line of horseback riders ambles along the trail far below. Not the swift express rider burning the breeze, but city slickers plodding along

T.M. on the Garstin Trail

on toy horses. A question occurs to Mom. What is the etiquette if one were to meet a horse, face to face, on the narrow footpath?

T.M and I forge ahead instructing her to just step aside and give the right of way to the horses. Peering down the steep canyon, the comment is, "Where do I step aside to?"

The answer is the "uphill side" as we climb higher away from the whoosh of cars in the city. T.M. points out our sweeping view including the Indian Canyons, the white granite dome of Tahquitz Peak and Red Tahquitz farther on the horizon. Landmarks are his specialty.

Identifying the Teddy bear cholla, I point out to him how the brown and fuzzy bottoms give them an appearance of a bear. The shorter cacti cluster around taller ones, like cubs under a mama bear. But don't try to cuddle. Not wanting to forget the faces of peaks and plants like acquaintances met at a party, we endeavor to remember their names for the next time we meet. Red spiked barrel cactus, once eaten, today is a botanical visual treat.

At eye level with a soaring crow-sized Cooper's hawk, we survey the Coachella Valley. The hawk is curious, making short flaps toward us then retreating, gliding into the next canyon, perhaps in search of a mourning dove meal. The Indians named the canyon for the hawk.

Francisco Patencio, oral historian of the Cahuilla, recalled the Pony Express subsidiary serviced Palm Springs for a short time. By routing through the valley, riders avoided the winter snows of the mountains and by following Indian trails, were provided food and water at villages. The hardy native mustang had the endurance needed for these bone-jarring runs.

One tragic day two renegade Indians ambushed the last valiant rider, robbing him of gold pieces, saddle and his life. He was attacked while passing through Hawk Canyon, later called Robber Canyon. The outlaw Indians, Andreas of Seven Palms and Venturo of Stubby Creek, were eventually caught and killed. Subsequently, no one ever was so bold as to take up the local Pony Express post again. Thus ended the Pony Express days in the Coachella Valley even before the telegraph finished the job elsewhere.

At the plateau on top of Smoke Tree Mountain, a cairn of piled rock marks a junction. The maze of trails coming together here tells of the importance of these routes to us now as well as in the old days. Here, travelers have many options, one of which is to follow the Wild Horse Trail to the top of Murray Hill, once important as a lambing spot for wild mountain sheep.

Berns and Araby Trail

The Garstin Trail ending, the Berns Trail leads us to the Araby Trail. Zigzagging along the switchbacks, my mind tracks back again to the Pony Express days. The route of these fearless horsemen was: Yuma to Chuckwalla Valley to Dos Palmas, El Toro to Indian Wells and Agua Caliente (Palm Springs) to White Water Point. Stops at Gilman's station (Banning) and San Bernardino were made before continuing on the urgent trip to Los Angeles and San Francisco.

Today, Hawk Canyon is known as the Araby tract, 80 acres south of Highway 111 at the base of Smoke Tree Mountain between Palm Springs and Cathedral City.

On Highway 111, below the Araby Trail, can be found an old Indian food-gathering place. "The place of worms," is where they came to harvest fat, wriggling armyworms. The banded or multicolored caterpillars were gathered like wild berries; plucked from the trees and plants they were consuming, they were eaten at great feasts. The leftovers were dehydrated and stored away whole or ground into flour. Yum. Yum.

Bob Hope Home

From the trail, one home stands out in a sea of sun-brightened white roofs. The roof matches the desert-varnished brown of rocks lying askew on the hillside like flattened tombstones. The gigantic mushroom shape of the roof seemingly grows. Bob Hope's fifties-style modern home dwarfs the other palatial mansions, one of which once belonged to movie star, Steve McQueen. Homes can no longer be built on the mountain.

Numerous no trespassing signs posted around the Bob Hope home clank in the wind. We, on the trail, pass the auditorium-sized landmark home. The Hopes, when in town, occupy their cozy bungalow downtown.

The Araby Trail ends unceremoniously, dropping into the backside of the Horizon Mobile Park where the hard pavement of Highway 111 hurts our feet.

The romance and myth of the Old West echoes in these mountain trails. What happened to the undelivered mail carried in the mochilla, the leather knapsack thrown over the rider's cinched-down saddle? Was there a sweetheart waiting to hear from her beau? News of a gold strike to a father awaiting word of a wayward son? The Old West, a symbol of fresh starts and impossible dreams, still echoes in hearts throughout the world.

Travel notes

Follow Palm Canyon Drive South past Murray Canyon Drive and turn left on Bogart Trail. The trailhead is near the east end of the Bogart Bridge. This hike combines the 1.5 mile Garstin Trail with 893 elevation change with the 1 mile Berns Trail with 369 feet elevation change and the 1.6 mile Araby Trail with 827 feet elevation change for a total mileage of 3.8 miles which will take about 2-2.5 hours. The Araby Trail drops down to Highway 111 at the entrance to the Rim Crest and Southridge development. Arrange for a car drop or return to car walking along Highway 111.

The location of the Indian "place of worms" is just east of El Cielo and Palm Canyon wash where Southridge Drive meets Highway 111.

Pony Express Quick Black Bean and Tuna Pan Bagna
(No worms)

2 cups green cabbage, shredded,
2 tablespoons rice wine vinegar
3 tablespoons sun dried tomatoes in olive oil, chopped
1 stalk celery, chopped
1/3 cup red onion, diced
7 ounces of canned black beans, drained
One 6 ounce can water packed tuna

One 7–8 inch round Italian bread
3 tablespoons olive oil

- Marinate cabbage 30 minutes in vinegar and drain.
- Slice bread horizontally. Scoop out soft inside of top and bottom. Brush olive oil on insides. Layer on one side: sun dried tomatoes, celery, onion, black beans and tuna. Cover with top half and wrap tightly with plastic food wrap. Place heavy can on top to press down. Refrigerate. Can be made up to 2 days ahead.

Trail of Pulchritude

*Celebrity Bus Tour and Downtown Strolling Tour of Casa Cody,
Community Church, Korakia Pensione and the Ingleside Inn*

&⬥ Serendipitous Cobb Salad Sandwich

Reporter Ernie Pyle (no relation) in painting his colorful word picture of Palm Springs as he found it in the 1930s wrote: "Although most visitors to Palm Springs actually come only to visit and get a good shot of sunshine, it was the idea of Hollywood pulchritude out here that finally made Palm Springs known to every cow-puncher and telephone girl in America."

Embarking on the TRAIL OF PULCHRITUDE, we hope to track down some of this Hollywood pulchritude of the past and see if it still exists in today's Palm Springs.

Celebrity Tour

We board the coach of the Celebrity Tour promising us a "glamorous 1 hour tour, driving past 30–40 homes of Palm Spring's rich and famous movie stars and celebrities." With over 700 millionaires residing in Palm Springs, including the members of the Agua Caliente tribe, we expect our tour to be a spin past locked gates, inaccessible neighborhood enclaves and mansions far down long driveways.

To our surprise and delight, Bob and Dolores Hope have a modest home here purchased 55 years ago that is said to be one of their favorite residences. The more famous modern landmark home behind gates on the mountain, we are told, is now used for fund raising and entertaining.

An old directory of their lovely neighborhood would have been the A list of superstars of the Golden Era of Hollywood. The tour guide explains that many early Hollywood stars had contracts that didn't allow them to go far from the studios. Elegant, warm Palm Springs made a perfect getaway.

The bus passes the home of Jack Dempsey, the heavy weight fighter, who ran around his yard training for fights. An H on a fence marks the former home of the 46 million dollar heiress Barbara Hutton who died penniless. Some stars built homes and others lounged regularly at "the place to be seen", the swank El Mirador Hotel.

El Mirador Hotel

From the bus window, we see all that is left of the grand El Mirador Hotel, its reconstructed distinctive tower. Opening New Year's Eve 1928, the El Mirador catered to movie stars and business tycoons. Wealthy guests, with extensive wardrobes in steamer trunks, arrived by train for long stays. Greeted with Hollywood glitz by fancy uniformed bellboys, they later dined on fine cuisine.

El Mirador means "watch tower" and this tower was the background for many publicity shots featuring starlets. The pool was a beehive of social and show business activity with pulchritude galore. Lucille Ball, Dorothy Lamour, Claudette Colbert, Spencer Tracy and John Wayne were just a few in the handsome and beautiful crowd gracing the grounds and the tennis courts.

During World War II, El Mirador became a hospital treating wounded soldiers from battlefields around the world. After the war, the hotel lost its popularity. In 1973, the Desert Hospital, retaining some parts of the old hotel, was built where it had stood. The original building and tower burned in 1989 but the tower we see today was rebuilt from original plans.

Young Ralph Bellamy and Charlie Farrell loved to play tennis at El Mirador. There is an oft-repeated story that one day during a match Marlene Dietrich stormed out and accused them of hogging the courts. Undaunted, they pooled $400 each and built their own tennis courts, the world famous Racquet Club of Palm Springs on Indian Avenue. Tapping into the desire of movie picture people for exclusivity, the entrepreneurs Bellamy and Farrell began to draw stars by making their club invitation only.

The town was freewheeling with relaxed rules. Casual dress, shorts and pants, was "de rigueur." Showing up in a skirt immediately marked a woman as a first timer. Palm Springs became a very cliquey town "thick with stars."

Ruth Hardy Park

Circling Ruth Hardy Park, which honors the first councilwoman, our guide says we have her to thank for the spotlighted palm trees planted along Palm Canyon Drive. The popular park with a broad expanse of lawn surrounded by shaped jacaranda and olive trees, reflects her concern for aesthetics.

The bus takes us to an area called Las Palmas by crossing over North Palm Canyon Drive and heading west toward the mountains.

Las Palmas

While winding through the streets between Vista Chino and Alejo Road, the guide spiels out name after name after name of movie stars, writers, entertainers, business moguls, statesman, billionaires, producers, inventors, all renowned people as we drive the land of second, third and fourth homes, mostly former estates.

Well-satisfied and entertained by the professional tour, we later return by car to explore Las Palmas streets and neighborhoods leisurely. We hope to vicariously assimilate the romance of the movie screen on our own trail. Instead we find ourselves enjoying the architecture and admiring the grounds of the rich and famous. We notice a bike route follows much of the terrain and think this too would be a pleasant ride.

Welwood Murray Cemetery

In the car, we go round and round in the exclusive star-studded neighborhood; Dad's erratic U turns attracting a security patrol vehicle. Finally, we arrive at our destination, the small quiet place at the west end of Chino Drive. The patrol car tailing us speeds away, seeing we are only interested in the historic pioneer cemetery. Here is where Dr. Welwood Murray was interred in 1914. It was the first community cemetery for white settlers of Palm Springs. The Murray family allowed burials of other pioneers on the small parcel of land. Nellie Coffman and Pearl McCallum are buried here along with Councilwoman Ruth Hardy, Charlie Farrell and his wife. The Aqua Caliente Indians have their own cemetery. All other residents must be buried out of town. After glimpsing the final resting place of the city's pioneers in the cool of the evening, we return downtown still searching for more Palm Springs "pulchritude" in the other charming, historic and architecturally interesting places rumored to be "the in" places to visit now.

Casa Cody

From Palm Canyon Drive, we meander down Tahquitz Canyon Drive and turn left on Cahuilla Road near the Desert Museum. The beautiful cousin of the legendary Buffalo Bill, Harriet Cody, founded Casa Cody, at 175 South Cahuilla Road, in the 1920s. The gracious bed and breakfast owner invites us to look over the grounds of one of the cities' oldest operating hotels. She talks of the concern the first hotel proprietors had for their guests and the influence of women as early hotel owners in town.

Community Church

Continuing on Cahuilla Road, we reach the intersection with Baristo Road, and pass the landmark Community Church. The Gothic Revival features are unusual.

Korakia Pensione

Turning right on Baristo Road and then right on Patencio Road, we stop at the Korakia Pensione at 257 South Patencio Road. Passing through the Moroccan-inspired enormous wooden doors into the courtyard, we almost hear the chamber music of the literary and artistic colony which made Palm Springs a glamorous Mecca for artists in the 1920s and 30s and think we smell the smoke of Sir Winston Churchill's cigar wafting in the air as he paints in his art studio room.

In reality, we see two restored historic adjacent villas set with surrounding bungalows, guesthouses, gardens and pools. Young guests, perhaps budding creative geniuses, lounge in the courtyard. One villa was built in 1924 by Scottish artist Gordon Coutts and the other by early screen star, J. Carol Nash. As we leave, a calico cat lounges on the white stucco wall. Above, the stony walls of Mount San Jacinto add a magic backdrop to this charming Inn.

Continuing south on Patencio Road, we turn left on Baristo Road, make a right on Cahuilla Road then a left on Ramon Road to Belardo Road.

The Ingleside Inn

Stepping through the wrought iron gates from the street into the hideaway of the glamorous Greta Garbo, we find an Inn listed as "One of the world's 10 best," by TV show, Lifestyles of the Rich and Famous. The Ingleside Inn at 200 West Ramon Road at Belardo Road is an official historic site built as an estate home in 1922.

In 1936, Ruth Hardy opened the Inn furnished with priceless antiques, such as a bust of Petrarch's Laura, collected by the original owners of the house. Bungalows were added later for more guest accommodations.

Ernie Pyle may or may not have stayed here but he certainly would have found his "pulchritude." Greer Garson, Lily Pons, and more recently John Travolta, Marlon Brando and Goldie Hawn are said to have left their signatures on the guest register.

Returning down Ramon Road, we once more walk bustling Palm Canyon Drive. Though we have spent a day looking for the beautiful people, we have seen no stars. It is said that by the sixties Palm Springs lost its exclusivity, became a sort of everyman resort. But I believe our failure to find "Pyle pulchritude" is only due to the disappearance of the beautiful and famous from public hotel swimming pools, tennis courts and restaurants, most of them having retreated to solitude behind dark glasses, villa walls and private suites in the shadows of the mountains pressing close. But you never know, an occasional glimpse may still be had.

Travel notes

Contact Celebrity Tours for information on rates and reservations: www.thecelebritytour.com or 760-770-2700.

The El Mirador tower is located at the Desert Hospital, 1150 N. Indian Canyon Drive.

The Welwood Murray Cemetery is at the west end of Chino Drive. Picnic grills and tables are available at Ruth Hardy Park on Avenida Caballeros and Tamarisk Road.

On the strolling tour, Casa Cody is at 175 South Cahuilla Road: 760-320-9346. The Community Church is at 284 South Cahuilla Road. The Korakia Pensione is at 257 South Patencio Road: 760-864-6411. The Ingleside Inn is at 200 West Ramon Road at Belardo Road: 760-325-0046.

Serendipitous Cobb Salad Sandwich

The Cobb salad was created in 1936 by Bob Cobb, owner of the Brown Derby restaurant in Hollywood. Mom remembers eating at the restaurant in the 60s when the salad was served in a mound of finely minced ingredients. For a picnic, we have placed the salad inside crusty bread.

1 cup poached and diced chicken breast
4 slices cooked bacon, crumbled
3 Roma tomatoes, seeded and diced
½ Haas avocado, peeled and diced
1 tablespoon chives, chopped
½ cup watercress, chopped
3 cups greens, chopped
1 large hard boiled egg, chopped
1/3 cup blue cheese, crumbled
Baguette crusty bread cut into 6 inch pieces
or 4 crusty rolls

Dressing
¼ cup olive oil
1 tablespoon red wine vinegar
½ teaspoon sea salt
Freshly ground pepper

- Combine in a shakable container oil, vinegar, sea salt and pepper to taste.
- At the picnic site, toss salad ingredients with dressing. Split bread and fill with salad. Serves 4. Can be made ahead: scoop out soft inside of bread, fill with salad and wrap tightly with food wrap. Refrigerate.

Trail of the Peninsular Bighorn Sheep

Short jaunt up Bighorn Overlook Trail

ᶻᵃ P. B. and Jalapeno Jelly Sandwich

O n the TRAIL OF THE PENINSULAR BIGHORN SHEEP, the green grass of a manmade oasis abruptly gives way to the trailhead of the Bighorn Overlook Trail beginning behind the Rancho Mirage City Hall.

Big Horn Overlook Trail

The wind immediately lifts my straw lifeguard hat and Mom stops twice to run after her gold hat sailing away. A convenient bench on the short trail gives us a chance to catch our breath in the relentless wind. The sky holds a glorious pillowing of cumulus clouds spilling through the San Gorgonio Pass.

Reaching the top, we hold onto the stone ramada supports to keep from blowing off the plateau. Organic flowing triangles of mountains pile up one against the other in the distance. The sheltering ramada reflects the rich colors of the landscape with its rocks of brown, orange and white. With deep shadows carving the mountains, T.M. tries to focus the telescope on the summer watering hole of the endangered Peninsular bighorn sheep.

The strong majestic creatures are invisible today; their muted brown color camouflages them on the stony slopes where they live. They usually don't inhabit areas disturbed by humans. Keen-eyed mountain sheep are not easily surprised as their far sight extends five miles and

Bighorn Overlook Trail

their sense of smell and hearing is almost as finely honed. They are as agile as high wire performers using their hooves like clothespins; the outer edges are hard and sharp and the inside spongy.

Bighorn have inhabited western North America, migrating from Siberia over 10,000 years ago. Peninsular bighorn sheep, a race of desert bighorn, live in the Peninsular Mountain range from Palm Springs including the San Jacinto and Santa Rosa Mountains to Baja California in Mexico. The herd has been decimated to fewer than 280 in the United States portion of the range. In the last two centuries, grazing, mining, homesteading and the loss of habitat to sprawling urbanization has decimated the herds drastically.

With a life span of 10 to 12 years, the few remaining sheep are severely threatened by a declining birthrate, viruses possibly from domestic livestock, poaching and mountain lion predation. Only one-third of the lambs usually born near steep cliffs from February through May survive their first summer.

The California Department of Fish and Game, the Bighorn Institute of Palm Desert and the California State Parks keep watch on the herds. The hope is to insure survival of these creatures of the crags and crannies, a daunting task.

Our retreat from the wind leads us back down the path, easy even for some who are not as agile as the bighorn sheep.

Travel notes

Park behind the Rancho Mirage City Hall located between Country Club Drive and Frank Sinatra Drive off Highway 111. The trail begins at the upper parking lot.

With only a 140-foot vertical climb, it is moderate to easy and can be done in about 10 minutes. (.02 miles up and back)

P. B. and Jalapeno Jelly Sandwich

Hot Jalapeno Jelly
1 cup white vinegar, divided
5 seeded jalapeno peppers
½ habanero pepper (hot)
1 tablespoon cilantro
½ green pepper
3½ cups sugar
3 ounces Certo
Makes 4 cups

- In a food processor blend ¼ cup vinegar, peppers and cilantro. Process until liquefied.
- In a saucepan combine sugar and remaining vinegar. Bring to a slow boil. Add pepper mixture. Cook 5 minutes at a slow boil. Remove from heat and add Certo. Stir until well blended and pour into jelly glasses. Refrigerate. Can be frozen or bottled and sealed.
- Serve with peanut butter on baguette of French bread.

Trail above Rancho Mirage

Mountain biking and hiking Mirage Trail

❧ Stuffed Medjools

Highway 111 is a river of cars today, but at one time it was the dusty route of the stagecoach lines. In those days, stages skirted the Santa Rosa Mountains on their way to Aqua Caliente (Palm Springs) from Indian Wells.

In 1924, the area now called Rancho Mirage was named the Eleven Mile Ranch; here early pioneers grew dates, citrus fruit and grapes. In 1946, the Ranch changed hands and reopened as the White Sun Guest Ranch.

Mirage Trail

On this TRAIL ABOVE RANCHO MIRAGE, now the home of presidents and celebrities, we begin a 4-mile out and back trail. The eroded wide trail ascends foothills suffused with a golden light. T.M. and I peddle the gray road kicking up gravel as Mom and Dad walk behind. Quickly, we wind around a bend and turn away from the city.

This October day is cool and windy. In the east, angelic white clouds are backlit by the golden sun. In the west, gray clouds caught in the San Jacinto massif threaten to snow dust the granite face. Seasonal change is in the air.

The windows and roofs of the "toy city" below glitter. We roll higher up the trail into the bold mountains on our geared machines. T.M. reaches the top ahead of me. He waves with white clouds

Top of the Mirage Trail

billowing behind him, seemingly appearing in a dream. I join him on the small plateau bulldozed along with the road for an old abandoned commercial project.

We play tag on the way down, bouncing over rocks and passing happy bikers and hikers enjoying the cool weather and come upon Mom on her rock perch. Dad had already descended the relatively easy trail. Surrounded by very wiry plants about two feet high, she tells us they remind her of Halloween fright wigs. Svelte young women on workout hikes had passed her along with mountain bikers. Mentally criticizing these serious exercisers for not halting and drinking in the striking severe beauty of the place, she was mortified when one lovely girl in her leotard asked: "Have you seen the rainbow?" She had not.

Travel notes

In Palm Desert from Highway 111 go west on Fred Waring until it ends. Turn left and go .1 mile to the Mike Schuler/Hopalong Cassidy trailhead. There is parking behind the Target store. Go right along the Mike Schuler trail to the unmarked Bump and Grind trail. Continue on and at 1.7 miles, the Bump and Grind road makes a right hairpin turn. It continues up to a graded flat area. Return the way you came. The easy Mike Schuler Trail to the moderate Bump and Grind Trail is

3.4 miles roundtrip with a 615 foot elevation change. It will take 1-2 hours.

For an alternate loop trip, stop at the Bump and Grind hairpin turn at 1.7 miles from the start. Look to your left and take the unmarked Herb Jeffries single track trail. In .7 miles you will reach a four way junction. Bear left. It is another .7 to the parking area. This moderately strenuous 3.1 mile loop trail has some steep downhill and will take 1-2 hours.

Stuffed Medjools

4 ounces Pecorino Romano cheese
16 Medjool dates

· Thinly slice the cheese. Slit date to remove pit and insert thin slice of cheese. Other options for the trail are to stuff dates with dried cherries or cranberries.

Trail of Rosie,
a Peninsular Bighorn Sheep

*Santa Rosa and San Jacinto Mountains National
Monument Visitor Center, short garden hike
and more challenging Art Smith Trail*

ᴊᴀ Rosie's Bag Lunch Garlic Chicken Sandwich
and Cherry Pie Bars

Dead Indian Canyon is where we follow a compelling tale of the od-
yssey of a particular Peninsular bighorn sheep. Rosie the Bighorn
once lived happily here chewing her cud with other wild ewes.

She, born of a wild ewe, was abandoned by her mother. The biologists entrusted with her care tried not to domesticate her. After being
released into the northern Santa Rosa Mountains, she found the
bountiful eats and water given by people living in the Bob Hope
neighborhood near the Araby Trail much easier to get than foraging
for food herself. The handouts stopped when the biologists got wind
of her frequent Palm Springs appearances.

Rosie returned herself to the wilds and the biologists happily re-
ported her appearance here in Dead Indian Canyon. But rejected by
her own kind, she began following hikers begging trail food and finally ended up in town at a shopping mall. Removed back to the isolated lonely Santa Rosas, her benefactors hoped she would stay away
from civilization. Their hopes were dashed with reports that the private, gated Bighorn Country Club was her new grazing pasture. Rosie
had become the luncheon companion of construction crews and

bedded down at night with Country Club statues of bighorn sheep. Rosie was in trouble again.

It was decided by the Department of Fish and Game, the Bighorn Institute and the Living Desert that for her own good she should join the captive herd at the Living Desert just a few miles from her current stomping grounds. Mystifying her captors again, she disappeared from the quarantine in Deep Canyon only to return to the luxury neighborhood on the Bighorn Golf Course. Evidently she missed her luncheon buddies. Another quarantine, this time with a companion, successfully detained Rosie. Now, several years after her escapades, Rosie, "Queen of the Hill", still climbs the nooks and crannies of the Living Desert Reserve terrorizing the rams of the herd.

Visitor Center

On the TRAIL OF ROSIE, A PENINSULAR BIGHORN SHEEP along the Art Smith Trail, we begin at the Santa Rosa and San Jacinto Mountains National Monument Visitor Center with its wide-angle view of the Coachella Valley. Inside the circular facility, Mom presses the horns of an exhibit getting an informative message about the sheep. Outside, the short Desert Garden Trail winds through native plants to benches carved in the shape of animals set under welcome trees.

In 1990, the Secretary of the Interior declared the Santa Rosa Mountains to be a "National Scenic Area," one of only four such designated areas in the country. Enhancing their protection in the fall of 2000, President Clinton signed a law designating the Santa Rosa and San Jacinto Mountains National Monument. Most of the Santa Rosa Mountains and their watersheds are accessible only along the foot or horse trails. Protected thus from the crush of urban development in Southern California are: Native American cultural sites, Peninsular bighorn sheep, slender toed salamanders and the peace of the desert.

Desiring to venture deeper into Rosie's Santa Rosa Mountains, we pick our way up the Art Smith Trail marked ceremoniously by an inscribed shard of pink stone. Dad now enthusiastically accompanies Mom, T.M. and I, comfortable with his new walking stick, a help for his hip discomfort while hiking.

Art Smith Trail

Art Smith Trail

The trail skirts a broad wash edging the left flank of the mountain; soon a plod through the sand and rock of the wash is necessary. Today we cheerfully trod along as transparent green and gold smoke trees light the way. The peaks reflect golden-orange and cream streaks. The deep baked-brown canyons walls thrust mightily at acute angles. Recent rain has rejuvenated the creosote bush to a bright olive green and the brittlebush leaves are the color of sage again.

The one-way 8-mile trail connects State Highway 74 at Dead Indian Canyon with other Palm Canyon trails. Our intention is to hike out and back only a portion of this one named for the trail boss of the Desert Riders.

The sloping ridges interlace, locking us into isolated Dead Indian Canyon. After 20 minutes in the wash, the trail begins to climb away from the main canyon. Deeper and higher into the desert Santa Rosas we step, achieving height very quickly.

Note-taking Mom sits on broken granite, swatting obnoxious gnats. We look back at the dry wash where in the not too distant past tumultuous torrents of water must have tumbled carrying the rocks we see strewn below. Teddy bear cholla cacti, like sentinels on guard over their territory, view our ascent up the trail. Shadows still darken the green and brown humpy ridges so prominent above us. T.M. and I press higher, leaving Dad pointing out the breakdown of the rocks into sand. "Sand," he declares, "is the element fueling the engine of the electronic industry." Soon, they are small figures picking their way back through the wash.

A cloud moves along in a mares tail over the ridge in a royal blue sky. At our first outlook point, we survey Rosie's favored Bighorn development watching the bulldozers at work. In a little over 1 hour, T.M. and I reach the first little oasis of small, squat fan palms nestled near their taller companion palms. It is ten degrees cooler and the scent of desert lavender is in the air.

Droppings and cleft hoof prints along the trail could have been from Peninsular bighorn sheep, perhaps the very ewes that ran Rosie off when a lamb was about to be born.

"Do you hear that?" T.M asks. I stop and we listen. Whack—whack—whack—it sounds like a rock hound rhythmically pounding away, yet we encounter no other human for the next 6 miles of trail.

The unseasonably cool weather and breeze propel us on. Another series of fan palms step up the steep canyon. T.M. becomes a tiny figure moving swiftly across the landscape. I lag behind marveling at how the fine shades of blue-green, sage and olive greens combine with the orange burnished tones of sand and rock to make an impressionist painting.

Reaching a plateau, we parallel distant Haystack Mountain. Though the desert beckons us on, we think of the 6-mile return trip and turn around. The Teddy bear cholla welcomes us back. After the sharp rocks of the trail, the wash feels soft and welcome under tired feet. We finish the 12 miles in 4 hours with the last sip of water.

The northern flanks of the Santa Rosa Mountains are deep, quiet and stark, just the sort of place Peninsular bighorn sheep need; that is except Rosie who prefers the city and the company of humans.

Some research later at home solved the mystery of the sounds we heard on the mountainside. What we had been fortunate to hear was the head banging of the curled brown horns of two jealous rams, endangered Peninsular Bighorn Sheep. Bighorns with their keen eyesight and acute sense of hearing normally would have been long gone when intruders approached but in the rutting season all attention is focused upon finding a mate.

Travel notes

From Highway 111 in Palm Desert take Highway 74 (Palms to Pines Highway) 3.7 miles to 51-500 Highway 74. The Visitor Center is open daily from 9 a.m.- 4 p.m. Closed Thanksgiving, Christmas and New Years day. Summer hours are 8 a.m. - 3 p.m. Information: 760-862-9984. The easy Randall Henderson loop trail is 2.4 miles with 423 foot elevation change and will take about 1 hour.

The strenuous Art Smith Trail hike described here goes 6 miles out and back for a total of 12 miles and will take about 6-7 hours. (The entire Art Smith Trail is 8.3 miles one way with a 1,465 elevation change.) The Art Smith Trail is subject to closures.

Rosie's Bag Lunch Garlic Chicken Sandwich

4 boneless, skinless chicken breasts
2 teaspoons dried thyme
2 tablespoons extra virgin olive oil
1 head garlic
¾ cup dry white wine (such as Sauvignon blanc)
Kosher salt to taste
Fresh ground pepper or cracked peppercorns

· Par boil whole garlic 3–4 minutes in boiling water until softened, drain and peel. Sprinkle chicken with salt, pepper and thyme. Sauté in olive oil until lightly browned in heavy pan. Add garlic and wine to pot. Cook over medium heat turning occasionally for 20 minutes or until pink is gone. Refrigerate.
· Serve cold on a whole grain bun. May spoon garlic on top. If desired add lettuce, Swiss cheese or sprouts.

Cherry Pie Bars

1½ cups flour
1 teaspoon baking powder
¼ teaspoon salt
3 tablespoons butter, room temperature
1¼ cups brown sugar
1 egg
1 teaspoon vanilla
2 tablespoons milk
¼ cup sliced raw almonds
¼ cup dried cherries

- Cream butter and sugar together until light. Beat in egg, vanilla and milk. Sift together dry ingredients and gradually stir into butter mixture. Add cherries. Spread in greased 8x11 pan. Sprinkle with almonds.
- Bake at 350 degrees for 20–25 minutes until golden brown.

Trail of the Living Desert

Living Desert Wildlife and Botanical Park in Palm Desert

ॐ Zesty Cabbage Deli Sandwich

Reno, the mountain lion, smiles a toothy grin showing off yellowed incisor teeth. "Please stay," is his silent plea as our tour guide hurries us away from his home in Eagle Canyon in the Living Desert. He is irresistible but still a wild animal, beautiful and fascinating to watch, a good ambassador for the desert. This Wildlife and Botanical Park is a sanctuary and outdoor classroom designed to deepen the understanding of the complicated and fragile desert in an entertaining way.

The Living Desert

Summer hours in July bring us to the park at 8 a.m. with the temperature already 95 degrees. In the heat, on the TRAIL OF THE LIVING DESERT, we try something new for us. Instead of walking, Mom, Dad, T.M. and other guests take the guided 50-minute electric tram ride.

Seated on the tram, our guide informs that we are in a rain shadow desert. Surrounded on three sides by mountains, rain clouds no longer retain moisture when they reach this desert. Occasional cloud bursts cause water to rush down canyons, over alluvial fans (fan-shaped sediment forming at the base of narrow canyons onto a flat plain at the foot of a mountain range) and crash through dry riverbeds. Passing a smoke tree in a wash, she explains that floods are a good thing for this tree. It cannot propagate unless its seeds are washed down a stream, crushed against rocks and germinate in the wet sand.

Eagle Canyon

Hauling around a corner, the first stop is the botanical gardens. She pulls the car close to a creosote bush enabling us to crush a leaf to smell the aroma of this plant, the distinctive scent of the desert. With this scent in our noses, we pass through Mohave, Upper Colorado and the Yuman desert garden with its organ pipe cactus.

The sand dune exhibit explains how these scalloped sculpted mounds are created by forceful winds funneling through the San Gorgonio Pass, sweeping sand from the Whitewater River at the head of the pass. Only a few of these wind-carved natural monuments are left in the Coachella Valley. A jackrabbit with enormous ears enlivens the scene.

Eagle Canyon, the next tour stop, brings our delightful encounter with Reno, the mountain lion. The guide explains he has come to know and enjoy the visits of hundreds of students on field trips. He has learned his grin attracts people to stay longer. Quickly, we pass through bobcat and Mexican wolf exhibits on our way out of Eagle Canyon to the desert Bighorn sheep. Feeding time has brought the elusive sheep down from the heights to peer at us. Is the wayward Rosie among them?

Giving right of way to a crossing squirrel, our driver brings us to the Arabian oryx; its horns gave rise to the myth of the Unicorn. Gazelles, Grevy's zebras and bat-eared foxes represent the African sector. At the turn of the road we pause; unlovely wart hogs are visible but the cheetahs are hiding. A swing by the African vulture aviary brings us face to face with a pair of tall, regal, endangered vultures intent on staring us down. Meerkats of Lion King fame perform before us as we return to our place of departure right on time.

On foot, we return to examine the Cahuilla Indian Ethnobotanical Gardens. The desert provided most necessities for a good life: narrow, straight arrowweed was shaped into arrow shafts by hunters; white sage crushed under their arms masked human odor; grayish-green yerba mansa growing in leafy patches provided relief for stomach ailments. The white flowered datura, a powerful hallucinogenic plant, induced trances in shamans long before recorded history. Tubular dull red flowers of the chuparosa gave sweet nectar. Desert agave, a staple food, provided flowers to parboil and leaves to bake. Bundles of deer grass were woven into baskets. Mom comments so many of the plants were used for stomach ailments. Digestive problems from their diet?

Inside the garden stands a reconstructed large "kish," a traditional Cahuilla home. Supported by a center pole, the walls and roof are thatched with dried palm fronds.

A quick trip through a dark, cool building concealing scorpions, bats, black widows and snakes brings us outside where we are invited by a docent to touch the back of a disabled Chuckwalla. This wide-bodied reptile sports the green, orange and brown color of the prevalent rock lichen where he grew up.

Above the Living Desert, Eisenhower Peak rises 1,952 feet. On a cooler day the Living Desert's Wilderness Trail is a treat. A 5-mile loop climbs to the 1,000-foot level of the mountain to a shady ramada.

Interested in desert landscaping, we stop at the Palo Verde Garden Center, which is open to the public. "Olla Bob", the Park's plant propagator, suggests planting a Mexican Paloverde tree in our coastal xeriscape garden. Enthused about our interest in the sweet-smelling creosote bush, he says that this once most common plant, rapidly disappearing due to housing development, is back in vogue.

Village WaTuTu Petting Kraal

"Do you like dates?" he queries and hurries away to some unseen place, returning with a box of dark brown Medjool dates freshly picked from the Park's own tree. The best ever. With creosote, ocotillo, Texas ranger bush and palo verde tree in our arms, we depart promising to inform him of their progress on the coast.

A walk through this living color encyclopedia of the desert teaches us and future generations to care for the valuable desert. Ambassadors like Reno with his lonely toothy grin and winning smile brings us back year after year to one of the country's premier botanical and wildlife parks.

POSTSCRIPT: While doing this update, I got to thinking how important the Living Desert was to me in learning the complicated, yet simple, story of "the wind, the sun, the sand and the little water, that created this special desert. And that is the theme of the new interactive Discovery Center adjacent to Marilyn's Merry-Go-Round and across from the peninsular pronghorn exhibit in the smoke tree wash.

I also got to thinking about some of my favorite memories at the Living Desert. Reno has passed away at the miraculous age of 22 but we will always remember this mountain lion's toothy greeting. Now, it's Salem, the female mountain lion from Oregon that ambushes us as one of the first visitors to Eagle Canyon. (I think summer admission at 7 a.m. is the best benefit of being a member.)

I was trying to decide what were my favorite memories in the last twenty five years. Maybe the hours spent in the petting kraal with rubber brushes in hand while two generations of kids brushed two generations of sweet-tempered Nigerian dwarf goats. Or the time detailed in this chapter when Bob Linstead helped us choose our Mexican Palo Verde tree. It's two stories tall now and thriving in our yard on the coast. Or the time we waited on the platform as the docents rang and rang the bell but the giraffes just decided not to come. Or was it the morning we seemed to be the only visitors in the park observing the bewildered and wet camels and other animals standing out in the rain?

I got to thinking also about some of my favorite places that were off the beaten path, like the Sonoran or Oasis ponds. And about the day I hiked the

Middle Loop out toward Eisenhower Peak alone. (And it became the setting for the ending of my historical fiction novel, *Dawn Breaks in the West.*) Then there was the time we were in the African Village trying to find the Baobab Tree (from the Little Prince) and when we inquired where it was we were standing right next to it. And the times I sat in the Cahuilla Kish in the Indian ethnobotanical garden just to listen to the wind blowing through the palm fronds or the magical day there I found myself in an eyeball to rotating eyeball staring contest with an orange skimmer dragon fly balanced on the tip of a bulrush. Or maybe the time inside the Tennity hospital where I held a hedgehog in the palm of my hand. And outside the hospital, the first time I saw beautiful Dewey the Acorn Woodpecker as he took my attention off the antics of Spot the Antelope Squirrel by tap tap tapping on his display window next door. I thought about how there was comfort in knowing that all the injured birds and animals are given the very best of care.

Also, I couldn't leave out the visits where I learned about the chuckwalla, the kestrel and the carpenter bees from the docents. I could go on. Let me just say, the Living Desert for me continues to be a constant renewing source of joy, inspiration, understanding, knowledge and good memories.

Travel notes

To reach the Living Desert Wildlife and Botanical Park from Highway 111 in Palm Desert turn south on Portola Avenue and proceed 1.5 miles to the entrance at 47-900 Portola Avenue. Admission fees: adults $12.75, seniors $11.25, children 3-12 $7.75. The park is open daily October 1-May 31 from 9 a.m.–5 p.m. and June 1-September 30, 8 a.m.–1:30 p.m. Closed Christmas day. Information: 760-346-5694 or www.livingdesert.org.

For hiking, ask for wilderness trail system sheet at the information booth. There are two trails leading to Eisenhower Mountain that form a loop. The moderate 5 mile Eisenhower Trail has a 689 foot elevation change and will take 3 - 4.5 hours. For shorter hike options try the .5 mile Inner Loop or the 1.6 mile Middle Loop which includes an informative highly recommended San Andreas Fault exhibit.

Zesty Cabbage Deli Sandwich

½ head green cabbage, thinly sliced
3 tablespoons Italian style olives, pitted and chopped
2 tablespoons olive oil

2 tablespoons rice wine vinegar
2 tablespoons water
1 clove garlic, minced
½ teaspoon sugar
Baguettes, cheese and meats of choice

· In a small bowl whisk together dressing ingredients. Add to cabbage and olive mixture. Toss and add salt and pepper to taste. Can be prepared ahead and refrigerated.
· Cut baguette into 4 lengths. Layer cabbage, meats and cheese. Wrap tightly in food wrap and refrigerate. Serves 4.

Trail of Toro and Santa Rosa Peaks

Drive up Santa Rosa Mountain Road, Short hike to
Santa Rosa Peak and Mountain Bike ride down mountain

                          ❧ California Muffuleta

C an mountain peaks be shape shifters, tricksters playing with travelers attempting to venture too high? On our first attempt to reach the tallest peak in the Santa Rosa range in April, a freak storm had dumped snow in rivers of white down deep ravines. At 7,000 feet, deep ruts in the snow on the steep road turned us back. This hot September day finds us under blue skies trying again to reach Toro Peak's 8,716-foot mysterious heights.

Winding by car 19½ miles up the Palm to Pines Highway 74 from Palm Desert, T.M. and I reach its junction with the Santa Rosa Mountain road marked with a large red wooden sign. Mom and Dad have decided to forego this bumpy twisty ride up a dirt road.

On the TRAIL OF TORO AND SANTA ROSA PEAKS, the road takes us into a land of ribbonwood and manzanita. Only a painter could do justice to the melding of brilliant colors.

The first mile is the worst; ruts and potholes wrench the gut. By mile 6, the life zone gives way to a bower of weathered oaks and by mile 9; tall Jeffrey pines mingle with firs on shaded slopes. Epithets are scrawled on the rocks and written on the trees. "Rocks don't burn but trees and man will." Dire warnings from the erstwhile Arkansas preacher we had read about? Certainly not the usual Forest Service sign.

Rabbit Brush

After an hour of bumping along the rutted rocky path cut into the mountain in the 1940s, at mile 10, we limp to the side of the road with a flat tire. Santa Rosa calling the shots again?

As T.M. fiddles with the jack, I begin a unexpected leisurely roadside study of the forest. Crushing pine needles between my fingers releases an aroma of lemon and vanilla. The Jeffrey pines stand guard. A wild flower daisy with a delicate face the size of a quarter cheers me up. Perfection so small can easily be overlooked against the immensity of the pines. Blooming rabbit brush stains the open woodland with yellow. Hunters with bow and arrows but no deer across the hood of their Jeep stop to ask if we are OK.

The valley near Pinyon Flat swirls below in a smoky hazy brew. Up here at 8,000 feet, this is the coolest place in Southern California to have a flat. The unforeseen incident has caused us to forego a cross-country hike to Toro Peak for a saunter up the road to her near twin, 8,070-foot Santa Rosa Peak.

Santa Rosa Peak

At a three-way fork in the road, we ramble to the right. The woods silent except for our footsteps crunching, our setting is idyllic. Then the piercing sounds of a radio and distant voices tell us we are no longer in isolation. Campers claim the peak.

The flat beds of two old pickups hold several campers lying on mattresses. Four dogs bark at us. T.M. explains we have come to see Desert Steve's cabin. The friendly camper asks if we know him? We laugh to ourselves knowing Desert Steve Ragsdale came to the Santa Rosas in the 1930s, died in 1970 at the age of 87. In a way we feel we do know him from his roadside warnings and the story of his cabin on 560 acres of mountaintop.

Author picnicking on
Santa Rosa Peak

This individualist and pioneer of the desert hailed from Arkansas. An itinerant preacher with a feel for the future, he opened a gas station and lunch counter in the Chuckwalla Valley in the early 1920s, offering free water to the few and far between travelers. When the road to Desert Center was paved, Interstate 10 ran right through his now thriving enterprise. Desert Center later became the gateway for the southern entrance of Joshua Tree National Monument, now a National Park.

"All that is left is the two-story chimney," the camper points out. "The cabin burned down four months ago." Heedlessly, he talks of the fire they built just last night here and we wonder if the cabin burned because of another camper's carelessness. We had read Steve posted signs at the cabin: "Decent folks welcome" and "enjoy but don't destroy."

Disappointed that the pioneer's landmark cabin has disappeared despite Desert Steve's dire warnings, we walk cross-country away from the blackened chimney, climbing ridges and rocks to a private picnic haven. Here, we loaf on the rocks of Steve's lush green peak high above the somber palette of the brown desert below. Toro Peak, about a 1½ mile away rises toward the east then drops precipitously to the canyons below.

Mountains are cradles of myth and legend. According to Patencio, the Cahuilla called Santa Rosa mountain "Weal um mo." Yellow Body, an Indian cultural hero, sat down here to extract a troublesome cholla cactus spine from his foot. He threw the spine on top of a stone and it blossomed into a mountain. Weal um mo.

Toro Peak, from which we have been turned back twice, was taboo; a place of evil spirits. Today, the Indians own it and the summit is leased to the Marine Corps.

T. M finds a hawk feather and we joke saying our trip up the mountain could be a feather in his cap. A lone hawk, possible owner of the

Spring wildflowers

feather, soars, drafting off the air currents. A small gray bird swoops down and catches a black and yellow butterfly in his beak. Purple flower clusters lift their blossoms to the sun on finely branched Santa Rosa sage. Wind blows in the treetops.

Our long resting at its end, I am the lucky one who gets to vibrate, bounce and plummet on my mountain bike down the road while T.M. tails in the car. I go down past the pines out of the shadows quickly into the sunlit chaparral. Plumes of ribbonwood flowers have turned champagne gold and rust, tinges of fall. Thunderheads of afternoon clouds cause black silhouettes to play hide and seek on the green hills. Bike and car finish at the same time; 10 miles of bone-shaking road fun in 51 minutes. Later inquiry at the Idyllwild Ranger Station tells us that Desert Steve's cabin fire is still an unsolved mystery.

Were we led astray by mountain vagaries? Does Toro Peak twist the plot or was it just fate turning us in a direction we had not planned and did not resist. Perhaps we will find out when we test the upper reaches of "Weal um mo" once more.

(P.S. On Memorial Day we drove back up Santa Rosa Spring Road without incident and stopped at a junction below Toro Peak. Violet-green swallows swooped down overhead with a "chee-chee" call. We gazed up at Toro Peak and made ready to climb. But something about the intrusive microwave tower on its top made it seem less appealing to hike than taking the left fork in the road about .25 miles back to do a lower cross-country hike that also promised spectacular views of the Anza Borrego desert below. A woodpecker made a tat-a-tat-tat on the Jeffrey pine tree. Our hiking shoes crunched over fragile soil. The odd-shaped bladder sage and orange Indian paintbrush wildflowers bloomed everywhere. Blue butterflies lit on blue penstemon flowers. Looking down over the desert I couldn't help wondering if this wildflower splendor was also enjoyed by ancient Cahuilla Indians moving back and forth between desert and mountain—a gift from "Weal um mo" who had once more led us on an unplanned journey.)

Travel notes

Driving up the mountain requires a high clearance vehicle. Snow may be encountered in winter, early spring and late fall. From Palm Springs take Highway 111 and turn right on Highway 74 (the Palm to Pines Highway) in Palm Desert. Proceed up the Highway 19.3 miles to Santa Rosa Spring Road on the left. Drive up the road and at mile 10 park and walk or continue driving the one mile up to Santa Rosa Peak.

Toro Peak has a locked gate and is no longer open to hikers or cars without permission from the Cahuilla Band of Indians.

California Muffuleta

½ cup pitted and chopped oil preserved black olives
⅔ cup green olives, chopped
2 tablespoons cilantro, chopped fine
2 tablespoons capers, drained
2 cloves garlic, minced
1 teaspoon dried marjoram
½ pound Provolone cheese, sliced
½ pound ham or turkey ham, sliced
½ pound Genoa salami, sliced
6 large bakery buns or crusty baguette

- Mix together black and green olives, cilantro, capers, garlic and marjoram.
- If desired brush bread halves with olive oil. Spread olive mixture on one half of each bun. Top with cheese and meats. Press down slightly.
- To make day ahead, use crusty baguette, scoop out soft bread, layer filling and wrap tightly in plastic wrap. Serves 6.

Trail of the Pinyon Pine Tree

Mountain biking Pinyon Flats Trail

🥑 Anza Valley Guacamole

Cahuilla clans gathered peacefully at Pinyon Flat, where the boundaries of their territories met, to harvest pinyon nuts and hunt game. Camping for a short time, they would undertake the arduous task of ascending the trees and batting the pine cones with sticks to free them. Gathering loosened cones stained hands with sticky sap. The cones were then dumped into a hot sand pit and roasted overnight. In the morning, the roasted cones were removed from the pit and beaten on a rock to force out the oil-rich seeds, which were ground into a meal and mixed with water for a gruel and a drink.

THE TRAIL OF THE PINYON PINE TREE has us balancing and pedaling on two wheels not to gather pine cones but to ride through the forest of small bushy resinous trees called pinyon pines.

Pinyon Trail

We start on the side of the road at the entrance to the Pinyon Flat campground, a block from Pinyon Drive. Exploring for a future stay, we make a loop around the small campground. Although close to the highway, we find the unoccupied sites pleasant with inviting picnic tables and fire pits under the shade of the pines. Back at the entrance to the campground, a marker begins the trail.

At an elevation of 4,000 feet, the temperature is 77 degrees and a cool pine-scented breeze blows. With this stimulant lifting our spirits,

Pinyon Pine Trail blowout

we peddle along dry rocky foothills into a grove of short-trunked pinyon pines with their compact crowns of green.

The erratically produced but valuable food crop, shared on common ground, drew Indians on a "first come first pick" basis from the villages. Pinyon nuts even today are enjoyed raw, toasted or as an ingredient in sweets and on pasta and salads.

At .73 on our odometers, we come to a dirt road, Palm Canyon Drive. We pick up the single track trail again across the road at a diagonal marked by a medium sized rock. We roll along a twisty, snaky trail. At 1.7 miles on the odometer, we note a rock cairn marking a short trail up to the road; we will follow it on the return trip.

Wheeling along, we begin a series of short steep uphill climbs, moderately steep declines and some hike-a-bike sections. San Jacinto etches itself into the distant horizon against a somber sky. Palm Canyon is a dry golden alley leading to the promised land of Palm Springs.

Pinyon pines stand leafless with blackened trunks and branches; evidence of fire. The ubiquitous ribbonwood, large evergreen shrubs that give these lower mountains their predominantly olive-green hue, are soft to a biker's leg. But highly flammable, the red shanks as they are also called, have been burned but recovered faster than the pinyons. Their plumes of white flowers bloom but the bark is still green. When mature, they will have the characteristic red-brown bark shredded like ribbons.

Our bikes charge ahead as legs pump. Armed with extra tubes for possible cactus spine-caused blowouts, we don't anticipate T.M.'s chain will break today. I peddle on alone finding the roller coaster ride on the rugged trail intoxicating. A reluctant return finds the chain fixed.

We head back to the cairn spotted 1.7 miles into our ride. This marks the quarter mile trail through a home development to the Pine Smoke Road. At the junction with the road, an unchained Rottweiler follows us with his eyes from his yard. Silently, we peddle the dirt road thinking—stay boy, stay. And he does.

After reaching Dunn Road, we turn right, Asbestos Mountain at our backs. Asbestos Spring was an important source of water for those harvesting pinyon nuts. Unlike the days of old when all the land was open, this area is now developed and defended.

At our approach, an owner working in her yard begins frantically calling her dog. Another—*gulp*—Rottweiler charges full speed showing a mouthful of teeth. Cringing, I peddle faster. The dog, capable of leaping the gate, runs toward us snarling and glaring. Reluctantly at the last minute he obeys her command and backs down. Relieved, we turn right onto Palm Canyon Drive and find safe haven through the dogless woods on the single track to our car.

Though tired and slightly threatened, we are thrilled to ride in this pinyon forest gathering knowledge and beauty. Rolling under the pines deep into the ribbonwood, one comes to know the essence of the green Santa Rosa face.

Travel notes

From Palm Desert, drive 15.3 miles up Highway 74 (Palms-to-Pines Highway), turn right at the Pinyon Flat campground and park outside on the side of the road. At the entrance to the campground, turn right onto a wide single track marked by a trail sign. At .73 on your odometer you will come to a dirt road. This is Palm Canyon Drive. Pick up the single track trail again across the road at a diagonal marked by a medium size rock. At 1.7 miles on the odometer note the rock cairn. When you have ridden as far as desired, this is an alternate route to return to your car. The cairn marks the ¼ mile trail to Pine Smoke Road through the home development. When you reach Dunn Road, turn right. Asbestos Mountain will be at your back. Turn right onto Palm Canyon Drive and then back on the single track through the woods to your car.

This trail eventually hooks up with the Palm Canyon Trail that extends all the way to Hermits Bench and trading post. The Aqua Caliente tribe does not allow biking in the lower canyons. Using Dunn Road beyond the locked gate requires permission.

Anza Valley Guacamole

We find the delicious fresh produce of the Anza Valley for sale at roadside stands. The local avocados, tomatoes and onions inspire this guacamole dip, a meal in itself.

4 medium Haas avocados, seeded and diced
2 medium vine ripened tomatoes, diced
½ cup cilantro, chopped
1 medium red onion, chopped
2 cloves garlic, chopped
2 tablespoons fresh lime juice
½–1 teaspoon kosher salt

- Gently stir together avocados and rest of ingredients. Add salt to taste. Serve with tortilla chips or inside pita bread.

Trail of the Desert Divide

Cedar Spring/Jo Pond Trail to Garnet Ridge

&. Easy Camp Pasta and Bruschette with Roasted Garlic

Standing on the great Desert Divide, the streets and landmarks of the Coachella Valley look to be a stone's skip away; Palm Canyon but a casual hike down. But this viewpoint is at an altitude of 6,400 feet; Palm Springs sprawls 12 miles away, 6,000 feet below.

To arrive at this outlook on the rugged spine of mountain separating the dry desert canyons from the dark brooding forest, we take our TRAIL OF THE DESERT DIVIDE, the Jo Pond Trail. Leaving Palm Desert, winding up Highway 74 (Palms to Pines Highway), we turn up paved Morris Ranch Road and park near Camp Joe Scherman, at the end of the road. The lush green Garner Valley charms with its expanse of white picketed horse corrals and picturesque gentleman farms.

On foot, we begin the Cedar Springs Trail, part of the Jo Pond Trail and one of the overlooked, less crowded paths that climb the southern San Bernardino canyons and ridges to the great Desert Divide.

The Jo Pond/Cedar Spring Trail

Threatening June rain has changed our plans from a two-day backpack to a day-hike to Cedar Spring and Garnet Ridge beyond. T.M. and I meander up a road past quintessential Californian groves of oak trees, latching and unlatching swinging gates as we walk. Delighted by a serenade of melodious bird songs but scolded by scrub jays for trespassing too close to unseen nests, we continue on. Rain clouds still hang like shrouds on the green rolling ridges. Our good fortune—the red Indian paintbrush and prickly pear blossoms have exploded with the recent moisture. Showy masses of yellow-orange flannel bush wildflowers have emerged.

Even in 55-degree weather, sweat soon soaks our clothing as the trail stops meandering and begins to climb. Zigzagging switchbacks up the ridge, we inhale the pungent aroma of the chaparral. Looking back, the high Garner Valley appears as a velvet green tapestry slashed with roads like cuts through fabric.

When the junction with the well-known Pacific Crest Trail running from Mexico to Canada is reached, we continue our trail on to Cedar Spring. Jet after jet breaks the silence, leaving trails of white in the still stormy sky. A patch of blue as big as a Dutchman's breeches, as my grandmother used to say, presages a pleasant day to come. The air feels warmer and dryer.

We now walk the rugged spine of mountain separating the dry desert canyons from the high mountain forests. These westward tilting granite mountains in the Peninsular Range have two diverse faces and both can be seen here. Their stark eastern desert face is golden, chiseled, seamed and wrinkled showing the bare bones of the earth at its lower reaches. In contrast, the western face is hidden, cloaked in thick green foliage. The mountains are a barrier to moisture reaching the desert.

Striding along the trail, we enter a sanctuary of black oak trees with furrowed bark and rounded crowns of spreading branches. Dusty-pink when leaves are unfolding, bright glossy green in mid-summer and yellow-orange in fall, these noble trees are slow growing, long-lived trees.

Passing through these lovely oaks, the myth of the ancient Cahuilla who ate the bitter acorns of this tree is recalled. A story tells of ancient times when the acorns were sweet but when Mukat, the Creator, became angry with the people, he changed the acorn to bitter. From then on, water had to be heated to leach the bitterness out of the acorns, a tedious task that fell to the women.

Dropping down the sloping contours of the desert side of the Divide, we soon reach cool Cedar Spring abuzz with mosquitoes. Lofty red-trunked incense-cedar trees shade a trickling spring. Surveying the campsite for another trip, we determine it to be well-cared for, with kindling wood left stacked for the next campers, probably by a group of Scouts. Logs around the fire ring serve as benches for lunch.

While T.M. filters water from the spring, I crush the scale-leaf of an evergreen conifer between my fingers releasing the distinctive scent of cedar. Highly prized, incense-cedar wood is soft but not splintery, desirable for manufacturing pencils. It is hard to imagine these towering trees reduced to number 2 pencils.

Two mountain runners burst into camp, having raced the same route as we have taken but arriving in less than half the time of our two-hour climb. Shortly, a lone teenager comes to dip water directly from the stream.

The Jo Pond Trail, named for a Desert Rider, threads another 12 miles downhill dropping 6,000 feet to Palm Canyon's West Fork Trail ending at the Hermits Bench and Trading Post in Palm Springs. The young man guzzling spring water shares his plans not only to walk all the way to Palm Springs today but there hop a bus for Las Vegas: "Make it a real adventure."

Pressing along this trail, we begin our final leg to Garnet Ridge. The soft-spoken polite young man not following the clearly marked trail sign disappears down an unmarked trail. We worry he may be attempting a dangerous bushwhack in a cactus infested, unforgiving stretch of land to the east.

Passing horse-watering troughs, we laugh. One tub has "no washin" scrawled across it but no horses drink or campers bathe in it today. Continuing on the Jo Pond Trail about another one-half mile, Garnet Ridge opens to unveil a drop to Palm Canyon below.

Turning back, retracing our steps to Cedar Spring, we are relieved to find our adventurer back at the campsite. Curiously, he has changed from heavy boots into sandals after following a game trail for a distance. He bows thanking us profusely for pointing out the right trail as we leave him at Cedar Spring to retrace our steps to the car.

Tired, eating French fries and pie at the Backwoods Inn, T.M. remarks that the young hiker still has a long distance to go. Will he make it down the grueling length of the trail? Is the bus station in Palm Springs open? Did he tell us his real destination? The practice of using trails dotted with springs to navigate between mountain and desert in Southern California is centuries old.

Travel notes

From Palm Desert take Highway 74 (Palms-to-Pines Highway) 24 miles to the junction with Highway 371. Go straight and continue on Highway 74 northwest for 4 miles turning right on Morris Ranch Road. Parking is available near Camp Joe Scherman, at the end of the road. Look for the trail sign on the right.

The 4.4 mile moderate roundtrip Cedar Spring Trail has a 1,326 foot elevation change and will take about 4 hours. The side trip to Garnet Falls is 1 mile and will take about 30 minutes on the Jo Pond Trail then return the way you came. The entire Jo Pond continues another 4.4 miles with elevation change of 4,553 feet beyond Cedar Spring to intersect with Palm Canyon's West Fork Trail to the Hermits Bench and the Trading Post in Palm Springs.

Easy Camp Pasta

2 pounds cherry tomatoes, quartered
4 ounces Kalamata olives, pitted and chopped
1 garlic clove, minced
2 tablespoons fresh basil, chopped
1 tablespoon olive oil
1 tablespoon white wine vinegar
¼ teaspoon sea salt
½ teaspoon red pepper flakes
5 ounces Feta cheese.
1 pound angel hair pasta

· Mix together tomatoes, olives, garlic, basil, olive oil, vinegar, salt and red pepper flakes. Pack in well-sealed container. Place Feta cheese in container.

- At the campsite, cook and drain pasta. Top each serving with tomato mixture and crumbled cheese. Serves 6.

Bruschette with Roasted Garlic

- At home, slice baguette of bread into ½ inch slices. Brush one side with olive oil. Place under broiler until golden brown. Cool completely, place in sealed bag.
- Slice off tips of the garlic head. Drizzle with olive oil. Wrap tightly in 2 layers of heavy-duty aluminum foil.
- At campsite roast head of garlic to the side of a medium hot campfire about 30–40 minutes until soft. Squeeze garlic from clove onto bruschette.

Trail of Romantic Old California in Ramona's Country

Hiking Cahuilla Mountain Trail

ᐓ Ramona Sandwich with Candied Grapefruit Peel

*I*t *was sheep-shearing time in Southern California....* Juan Diego, subject to occasional lapses in memory and erratic behavior, finished his day's work with the sheep and rode a sleek black horse home instead of his own broken-down old mare. Seeing the mistake he had made, his wife Ramona urged him to go back immediately and exchange horses. Juan needed to rest first and fell asleep. But vigilante justice ruled the West and came quickly.

When Sam Temple, an American settler, discovered his horse had been taken, he rode up the steep mountain trail to the Indian's home, emptied his double-barreled shot gun and six-shooter into Juan as Ramona watched, clutching their infant daughter. Horse stealing brought down the same punishment as killing a man and when the horse thief was an Indian to boot, one should not wonder that brutal Sam Temple from San Jacinto considered his cruel actions justifiable homicide.

Fate catapulted the lives and plight of these Southern California Indians into the national spotlight when facts of this murder ignited the imagination of poet, novelist and Indian advocate, Helen Hunt Jackson. Hoping to stir the consciousness of the nation like Harriet Beecher Stowe with Uncle Tom's Cabin, Jackson published her book in 1884.

The romanticized novel Ramona elevated the cause of the Cahuilla Indians, Ramona Lubo and Juan Diego, to heroic levels by creating fictional characters: a beautiful half-Indian, half-Mexican Ramona, and a dashing noble Indian, Alessandro. Readers were enchanted with Jackson's first hand account of Old California. This extraordinary woman traveled extensively in Los Angeles, San Diego and Riverside in the age of the stagecoach and steamship.

Juan Diego Flat and Cahuilla Mountain Trail

Pursuing this real TRAIL OF ROMANTIC OLD CALIFORNIA IN RAMONA'S COUNTRY and this sad chapter in Western history woven into nineteenth century literature, we follow a pastoral road from the town of Anza. Not in a stagecoach but in a car, we turn onto a dirt road flanked by tall ribbonwood chaparral. The Cahuilla Trail begins at Juan Diego Flat in a valley between Little and Big Cahuilla Mountain at 4,480 feet. The chaparral on the Flat is heavily charred from a recent fire that has also burned the trail sign.

The valley remains very much as Jackson described the setting for Alessandro and Ramona's home in the climax of the novel:

> ...a wondrous valley...the mountain seemed to have been cleft to make it. It lay near midway to the top, and ran transversely on the mountain's side...
>
> Gone is their small cabin with: "...walls of hewn pine and roof of thatch, tule and yucca-stalks double laid and making a sort of bower like veranda."

With only a few modern homes in the distance, a yellow dirt road cuts through the mat of varied green in the Cahuilla Valley. Raw landscapes of peaks now spin us in every direction: the peak of San Jacinto dominates 16 miles away, the uneven saddle of coastal Saddleback Mountain, Thomas Mountain and Santa Rosa Peak stretches across the skyline. Today, no wagonloads of star-struck romantics come to seek Ramona as they did at the turn of the century. Today, only we chase the ghosts of the past along our trail.

A spring hike on the trail awash in wildflowers or one in fall with its golden oaks would be ideal. But our summer trek has brought us to the mountain in 97-degree heat in a burned landscape.

Wisps of white clouds migrating from Mexican tropical storms give us some respite from the heat. Mountain lion and deer tracks lead us up the gently curving trail. Wild fire, like a dragon's breath, seems to have snuffed out the very life from the land.

As we climb up into the charcoal void, I can almost hear the shots ring out in the valley. Sam Temple, the killer of Juan Diego, was tried and acquitted. Eventually, caught up in the romanticizing of the story, he came to brag that he was the one who shot Alessandro, the fictional character. The fact and fiction intertwined in this story did culminate in important federal government intervention on behalf of the Cahuilla Indians simply by putting a human family's face on the tragedy.

With thoughts of the drama and its outcome, we walk through the desolate scene. Pine cones still hanging from blackened Jeffrey pines look like long-forgotten Christmas ornaments. Walking here brings feelings of loss but a wellspring of emerging green tells of renewal.

A hike of 1.5 hours brings us to a saddle, a ridge connecting two higher elevations, a few hundred feet below the summit. Untouched by fire, Jackson's description over one hundred years ago still describes it:

> *A short distance off a spur of the mountain widening out into almost a plateau. This was covered with acorn-bearing oaks and under them were flat stones worn into hollows where bygone generations of Indians had ground the nuts into meal." "Indians did not often now venture so high up as this. It was held to be certain death to climb to its summit and foolhardy in the extreme to go far up its sides.*

Heeding the Cahuilla advice, we stop short of the summit. Stone cairns, piles of quartz rocks, mark the end of a 930-foot vertical climb. Here, seated in the shade of a black oak grove, it is almost 100 degrees Fahrenheit but a breeze ruffles the leaves and our hair. Stickers burrow into socks and flies buzz.

Wanting to linger but bidding goodbye to the sheltering black oaks, we return the way we came. Distant blue peaks toss over the closer Santa Rosa Mountains cloaked with the lacy cream plumes of the ubiquitous ribbonwood.

The real Ramona Lubo was buried in 1922 beside Juan Diego in the old Cahuilla cemetery in the shadow of the Cahuilla Mountain, near the new Cahuilla Creek Casino. Her expert basketry became a very salable commodity to those coming to seek her out. What did Ramona Lubo say when people came to her expecting to see the beautiful Ramona of the novel?

The 5-mile hike behind us, wanting some local color and a cool treat, we head for the Stagecoach Inn in Aquanga. Munching French fries and eating ice cream while reading local history on the walls, it seems Aquanga means something like "water bubbling up." Sometime in the past an earthquake had stopped a seep here.

Just a few blocks from the Inn across Highway 79 and about 10 feet from the road, a marker catches my eye. I plead to stop and investigate. Here we find a bit of unexpected Western history.

U.S. soldiers known as the Mormon Battalion marched in 1847 through the area following Temecula Creek toward the ocean. Starting in Iowa and ending at San Diego, this cruel cross-country march that found the men often in dire predicaments, was the final segment of a 2,000-mile trek, the longest in U.S. military history. Picks and shovels wielded by these heroic men carved the first wagon trail built across the Southwest deserts into Southern California. Pioneers and settlers trudged this same trail. The Butterfield Overland Mail, an important factor in development of rapid communication between the East and Far West, drove it in light covered coaches high in speed but low in comfort. Near the Battalion marker is a head stone reading:

> Jacob Bergman 1832–1894
> Gracious Host Station Keeper
> Stage Driver U.S. Trooper
> "A House Beside the Road
> A Friend to Man"

Helen Hunt Jackson traveled this stage road, too. Though she died the year after Ramona was published, her spirit lives on in her immortal words and she still roams here free in the imagination of all who come seeking Ramona and Alessandro.

Travel notes

From Palm Desert take Highway 74, 24 miles to the junction with Highway 371. Turn left and proceed along Highway 371, 9.4 miles to Cary Road. Turn right (north) to a junction then turn left at 3.5 miles. Continue bearing left and drive up to Juan Diego Flat another 1.5 miles. Park in the clearing on the right side of the road under the overhead wires. Look for the Cahuilla Trail on the left. As of this writing there is no trail marker.

Cahuilla Mountain has now been designated part of a 5,585 acre Wilderness. This moderate 5 mile out and back hike has an elevation change of 1,100 feet and will take about 2-3 hours. For information contact the San Jacinto Ranger district in Idyllwild at 909-382-2921.

To reach the Stagecoach Inn in Aquanga, from junction of Highway 371 and Cary Road proceed northwest 11.1 miles along Highway 371. At the junction with Highway 79 continue west 2 miles on Highway 79 to the Stagecoach Inn.

The Mormon Battalion marker is several hundred yards before the restaurant on the opposite side of Highway 79.

Ramona Sandwich

In the 1890s, an issue of a ladies magazine published details of a "Ramona Luncheon," to honor the engagement of an Eastern girl to a boy of Spanish descent, inspired by Helen Hunt Jackson's romantic novel. This recipe is an adaptation of the published Ramona sandwich filling and is surprisingly good.

6 ounces red currant jelly
3 dried candied pineapple rings, coarsely chopped
6 dried figs, chopped
½ cup dates or raisins, chopped
¼ cup candied grapefruit peel,
coarsely chopped (see below)

- Fold ingredients into jelly. Serve on buttered white or brown bread. Serves 4–5.

Candied Grapefruit Peel

2 large Coachella Valley ruby red grapefruit peels
3 cups sugar, divided

- Cut grapefruits in half. Remove all pulp. Cover peels with cold water. Bring to boil and cook until tender pouring off water and adding fresh cold water several times. Drain. With spoon remove white inner portion of peel. With a scissors or knife cut peel into uniform ¼ inch strips
- Make simple syrup by bringing to a boil 2 cups sugar with 1 cup water. Add peel, cook over low heat until peel has a clear candied appearance. Remove peel strips individually from hot syrup and roll in 1 cup sugar until well coated. Cool on rack. Store in tightly covered container. Keeps for 1 month. Makes 1 pound.

Trail of Shangri-La in the Colorado Desert

*A visit to historic La Quinta Resort and Club Hiking
Bear Creek Canyon Trail out of La Quinta Cove*

ꝯ Turn of the Century Langostino Salad

Shangri-La. Everything is right with the world on the sun-drenched terraces of the La Quinta Resort. A secret hideaway, a muse inspiration is what Frank Capra, Hollywood film writer and director, found when working on the script for It Happened One Night here in 1934. The film eventually swept the Oscars. Superstitious about La Quinta as his lucky charm, he made it a habit to work here conceiving other smash successes like Lost Horizon, Mr. Smith Goes to Washington and Meet John Doe.

La Quinta Hotel

A long allée of perfectly matched Italian cypresses takes us on the TRAIL OF SHANGRI-LA IN THE COLORADO DESERT to one of the most unique places in the world, the oldest resort in the Coachella Valley. Our focus is on the real desert but we feel we have earned our respite from the burning July sun with a visit. Here we can spend morning, afternoon and twilight watching shadow and light play on the natural beauty of the Santa Rosa Mountains.

Our first visit over 10 years ago was a stroll after dark along lighted pathways of the carefully tended grounds surrounding the original 20 quaint casitas of authentic early California style.

As we check in today, the shaded portico and lobby look much as they do in old photographs from the 1920s. The visionary founders came to the desert for health concerns and purchased 1,400 acres of "Happy Hollows" as the Cahuilla natives called this land. La Quinta opened for business in 1926. The biggest stars of the Hollywood golden era arrived regularly in motorcars bypassing Pearl McCallum's Palm Spring's Oasis Hotel and Nellie Coffman's Desert Inn, to drive the sandy, hazardous 19 miles for the isolation and privacy of the resort. Regularly lounging in private casitas were stars like Errol Flynn, Clark Gable, Marlena Dietrich, Katherine Hepburn and Bette Davis. Even during the depression years, the stars came and La Quinta flourished.

Prohibition found guests sipping orange juice spiked with illegal spirits in the Santa Rosa room. La Quinta's guest register posted names such as Dupont and Vanderbilt and later President Eisenhower.

In the morning light, the mountains are surreal flattened forms with the sky a sheet of blue paper, a perfect background for breakfast at Morgans on the patio. The Plaza sprawls. Up in the courtyard heavy wooden chairs invite Mom to sit under a blue umbrella and admire the artfully crafted arched alcoves of the Salon de la Fiesta with its huge bell. Enormous Mexican carved doors will soon open for an event; the ambiance of an elegant old Spanish villa is complete with the pleasing splash of water from fountains and aqueducts. Festive bougainvillea vines, jacaranda trees and summer zinnias bloom, complementing carefully manicured old shrubbery.

Hotter than Hades at the pool with the afternoon sun beating down, I retreat to the shade of the patio with pen and paper hoping for Capra's muse to visit me but the heat drains away all ambition. The untamed mountains seem close enough to touch; crowds of dark brown pinnacles push up. I feel as if I could easily walk along the zigzag backbone. T.M. dives into the pool. Dad hibernates inside a cool room while Mom absorbs J. Smeaton Chase's, Our Araby, the 1920s guidebook of the desert. The rugged skyline of the Santa Rosas is softened by the golden sheen of the hazy afternoon. All sounds are deadened.

Later, as the gold sinks from the peaks and the reds die, twilight finds us rallying yellow balls on the grass tennis court. The ball becomes invisible in the air when the mountains turn a velvety purple. The gray light of night descends, shrouding the rims and creating a shadowland of bold black shapes. The seemingly immutable mountains are stealthily moving and changing, creeping with the eternal pressures of Mother Nature to return them to the flat surface of earth.

Bear Creek Canyon

After a day of lounging, a hike out of La Quinta Cove seems promising. A few miles from the hotel, we locate the Bear Creek Canyon Trail. Passing the bike path on our right, we follow the faint dirt trail to a stand of date palms. At 6:47 a.m., it is already 85 degrees. From a rock outcropping, we see the long stretch of wash that must first be trekked before one can reach the trailhead where the steep climb begins to rise over 2,000 vertical feet to the high country. With false bravado, I insist we begin, leaving Mom and Dad resting and remarking that the mountains today look like an ugly heap of randomly tossed debris.

T.M. and I crunch deep in the wash for almost an hour. Hopes for the high country goal sink as the sun rises higher; with too much wash to conquer, I surrender. Doing an about face after some recriminations from T.M., we resolve to return in the cooler months. We are left with a sympathetic feeling for those who in the past viewed mountains as menacing obstacles to be overcome and not benevolent providers of magnificent scenery. The saunter back to the refuge of La Quinta affords a sweeping view of the valley, making the short morning trek worthwhile.

Another day in the desert has passed with the nuances of the sun upon the Santa Rosa Mountains dominating the valley. The trickling fountains remind that water is the gift of life in the desert. Shangri-La, a paradise on earth, a hideaway of idyllic beauty and tranquillity, can be reached in the desert at the La Quinta Resort and Club.

POSTSCRIPT: We returned in March to hike the Bear Creek Canyon Trail to the Oasis. The brittlebush was in abundant yellow bloom and I ranked this trail as one of my all-time favorites. After we finished, we celebrated on the La Quinta Resort Plaza under the blue umbrellas with margaritas and delicious guacamole and chips. It was a memorable spring day.

Travel notes

The La Quinta Resort and Club is at 49-499 Eisenhower Drive in La Quinta. From Highway 111 go south on Washington Street then right on Eisenhower Drive. Information: www.laquintaresort.com. To reach the Bear Creek Canyon trailhead from Highway 111 go south on Washington 1.4 miles. Turn right on Eisenhower Drive and go 3.7 miles. Turn right on Bermudas. Follow another .3 mile until Bermudas becomes Tecate. Park at the corner of Madero and Tecate. At .2 you will reach the cove oasis ramadas and picnic tables. Continue straight (south) toward the rock formation. The trail is well marked and at the bottom of the small hill the trail goes left through the wash. In 2 miles the trail leaves the wash and begins to climb. It is about 2.5 hours to the oasis. This strenuous 9.73 mile out and back hike has a 2,287 foot elevation change and will take about 5-5.5 hours.

Other hike options from La Quinta Cove: From the parking area near Bermudas walk .6 mile until you reach the sign for the Cove to Lake Trail and Boo Hoff trail junction. Hike options here are out and back hikes of the length desired or a Cove to Lake/Boo Hoff Trail strenuous loop of 12.3 miles with 2,464 elevation change plus the 1.2 miles out and back to the parking area.

Dogs are allowed only out to the Cove/Boo Hoff trailhead.

Turn of the Century Langostino Salad

This turn-of-the-century recipe called for lobster. We substituted small sweet tender crustaceans, langostino tails, for an easy economical picnic.

1 pound cooked and peeled Langostino tails
Greens chopped very fine
Dressing
4 hard-boiled egg yolks
2 ounces canola oil
2 ounces red wine vinegar
3 teaspoons dry Colman's Mustard
½ teaspoon cayenne pepper
½ teaspoon sea salt
Croutons if desired

· Mash hard-boiled egg yolks with back of wooden spoon and whisk with rest of dressing ingredients. Rinse and pat dry langostinos. Top greens with langostinos and just before serving spoon dressing on top and toss. Serve with lemon wedges and crusty bread. Makes 2 large salads or 4 side salads.

Trail of the Ocotillo

*Lake Cahuilla recreational area,
challenging hike of Boo Hoff Trail*

♣ Fruits of the Valley Bonbons

Planning and plotting one's trail into the desert works only to a point. When serendipity, the unplanned, takes over, traveling ancient pathways becomes an adventure. We are drawn farther into the open stony slopes of the desert by clusters of vivid red flowers atop a siren plant.

Lake Cahuilla recreation area, the Morrow Trail

Parked under the palm trees at the Lake Cahuilla recreational area, our planned 9-mile Boo Hoff Trail becomes our TRAIL OF THE OCO-TILLO and adventure begins when T.M. examines the map and finds a miscalculation. Our omission of the 3 miles of connecting Morrow Trail will make for a much more strenuous journey of 12.3 miles. We press on with determination leaving our return open to making an out and back hike or alternatively, doing the full loop.

Under a thin veil of clouds, we strike out on the Morrow Trail. Soon the little clouds evaporate heedless of our long trek, exposing us to the full brunt of the April sun. Down in the breezeless gully, the late noon start immediately takes its toll. Slogging along the sandy wash, an endless sand trap, the harshest of footings, T.M. claims lost golf balls as trophies. This wash parallels a golf course.

Backs begin to straighten and feet become resigned to the unaccustomed difficulty and slowness of the path. The sight of hundreds of rusted cans and broken bottles, the souvenirs of the past practice of using the desert for target shooting, is distressing. Finally, a delicate quail's nest in a graceful paloverde tree gives hope for better things to come and distracts from the grumblings of the body and the misused land.

We rise like phoenixes out of the wash with sweaty clothes and hair to find we have reached the Boo Hoff trailhead. The unusual name Boo Hoff is dedicated to a Desert Rider instrumental in protecting and restoring these treasured Indian paths.

Boo Hoff Trail

This trail follows an ancient Indian path passing through Guadalupe Canyon and along the edge of Devil Canyon. Our moods change from irritation to delight. Now, with the gap between our world and the domain of the tall, prominent Fouquieria splendens bridged, our legs carry us effortlessly through a splendid ocotillo garden.

Blooming on a sea of brown rock, graceful waving stems like undersea coral whip in a waterless ocean. Wet soil providing the energy, tiny green leaf buds burst along stems and send tight clusters of scarlet tubular flowers up into the Sonoran sky. Other plants thrive in this landscaped garden of the gods; barrel cactus and the many-jointed Teddy bear cholla grow like bouquets of flowers. But the ocotillo, vestige of a more tropical time when the deserts where forming in North America, rules here.

Now at the halfway point of the loop trail, it is decision time; retrace our steps and finish in an hour or finish the loop in another 3–4 hours. Sand wash all but forgotten, senses heightened feeling the energy of the "ocotillo spring," I hear myself saying: "Let's do the whole loop."

Deeper and higher into the desert, we climb to a viewpoint where the Salton Sea is a small sapphire pool; snowcapped San Jacinto and San Gorgonio Mountains beacons behind us shining across the valley. The heavy silence of the stony slopes allows the language of the bees visiting the ocotillo to be heard. Completely alone, the miles roll along until our descent along the rim of Devil's Canyon is completed.

Back down in the wash once more, our boots slosh through dry sand and tiny pebbles. It is like walking up a river without water. Other

Ancient Indian Path—Boo Hoff Trail

hikers now have come up the wash and some explore in four wheel-drive vehicles. The penance of the wash completed, the pavement cruelly bruises our tired feet as we finish our 12-mile serendipitous adventure.

The returning shadows penetrate the crevices of the rugged mountains as we glimpse the last fingers of golden sunlight on the tips of the peaks. The unexpected length of our adventure leaves us spent but vividly aware of the siren plant that called us along this ancient trail. In a month or so the green leaves will turn yellow and drop. The brilliant flowers will become dusty and brown, falling to the ground as the sun wheels overhead. Ocotillo will wait for that infrequent rain promising many springs for her. Should you stumble into the desert in Ocotillo Spring, you, too, will be drawn farther than planned into their rocky domain.

Travel notes

To reach Lake Cahuilla from Highway 111 in Indio, go south on Madison for 5.6 miles. Turn right on Avenue 58 and proceed to the entrance station. Day use fee is $2. Open sunrise to sunset.

This loop trail begins at the trail head for the Morrow section of the Cove to Lake Trail which is directly across from the Lake Cahuilla Park entrance station. The loop trail combines the moderate 2.9 mile, 548 foot elevation change Lake to Cove Trail with the strenuous 8.8, 1,916 foot elevation change Boo Hoff Trail. At the end of this loop the Boo Hoff trail ends at Avenue 58. Turn left and proceed .6 miles down the road back to the day use parking area. This strenuous 12.3 mile hike with 2,464 feet elevation change will take about 6 hours.

Fruits of the Valley Bonbons

1 cup dried figs
1¼ cups golden raisins
1 cup Medjool dates, pitted
½ cup walnuts or pecans, chopped
1 teaspoon orange zest
1 tablespoon orange juice
1½ pounds white or chocolate candy coating

· Freeze the dried fruit for 10 minutes before chopping. Finely chop by hand or with food processor. Blend fruit and nuts with orange zest and orange juice. Roll into 1 inch balls. Refrigerate until set about 2 hours. Follow heating directions on candy coating package. Dip balls, coating generously. Place on wire rack to harden. Makes about 30. Can be frozen for later use.

Trail of the Fish Traps

Short walk to view ancient fish weirs, drive to Travertine Rock

ᔕ Easy Old-fashioned Raisin Sour Cream Pie

T HE TRAIL OF THE FISH TRAPS, ancient stone weirs, leads us on a fan-tastic voyage where we walk under a freshwater sea without getting wet and where petroglyph rock art whispers secret stories.

The fish traps were mysterious from the beginning for us. In an attempt to divine their location from a road map, we had come within a stone's throw of them. But not really knowing what Fish Traps looked like our efforts failed. Later, a docent at the Aqua Caliente Museum suggested calling the Bureau of Land Management. The traps still threatened to remain a mystery as bad timing found me standing bewildered in the BLM office getting nowhere. However, I was pleasantly surprised when the dedicated staff archeologist tracked me down by phone on a holiday and gave me specific instructions to reach the elusive Traps. There was much joking that evening about what they would look like? Were they like lobster traps or giant cages?

Early the next morning, anxiously following our directions from Indio, we come to a pedestrian gate near an agricultural field. Slipping through the gate, our route becomes navigation by landmarks. We cross a small stretch of private land to reach the tiny county park that is on the National Register of Historic Places. To the right is a small grove of citrus trees and to the left abandoned beehive boxes; just as the archeologist had said.

The dirt road follows the side of the mountain as we walk in our imagination under the surface of Ancient Lake Cahuilla. To make sense of all of this, we must go back in time geologically to when the last freshwater Ancient Lake occupied this Salton Sink area.

The Ancient Lake Cahuilla

Four to five million years ago, the warm aquamarine water of the Sea of Cortez extended out of present day Mexico all the way here to the Salton Trough. During the past two to three million years, many ancient lakes have filled the Salton Trough. At one time in the course of carving out the Grand Canyon, the epic force of the Colorado River flowing into the Trough carried tons of silt; this part of the Trough was dammed from the rest of the Gulf with a delta by about the late Pliocene Age. Landlocked and cut off from a source of water, the sea gradually evaporated.

The Colorado River would cut through the dam and fill the area with freshwater many times. It is thought that about five hundred years ago, the Colorado River changed its course once more and no longer provided fresh water for the lake. Indications are that the lake was present until about three hundred years ago. Evaporation and the dry desert climate caused it to dry up.

Above us the beach lines of the northwestern shoreline of Lake Cahuilla are clearly visible as watermark bands along the foot of the hills. In ages past, this enormous lake with a high water level at 42 mean feet above sea level would be lapping the rocks far above.

Out in the field a worker's radio pounds out a rock song and in a strange way the beat sounds like drums and the song like Indian chanting. Scanning the hillside, which would have been the shoreline, we remember the archeologist said to be on the lookout for Indian rock art on the unusual mushroom-colored tufa formations.

Indian Petroglyphs

At first the tufa seems to be scrawled only with modern graffiti but T.M.'s sharp eyes begin to pick out the petroglyphs, faint etchings of animals, webs and arrows. The petroglyphs are lasting symbols of an Indian culture without written language. The year 1877 is written on one tufa face. Is this a prankster or an authentic nineteenth century marking?

The organically-shaped tufa formations are believed to date from 900 to 1600 AD. Tufa or porous travertine is a variety of calcium carbonate commonly deposited along lake shorelines. Formations here could have resulted from lapping wave action and spray.

Fish Traps

Continuing down the dirt road, the right angle curve of the old shoreline, now a dry piling of rocks, is revealed. With our new information, we believe this could have formed a calm area or cove, a logical place for fish to congregate during storms. Hot wind brushes our cheeks, a reminder that the sea was not large enough to have tides but that wind did create waves and rough conditions in storms.

About one-fourth of a mile down the road, we reach the small berm, a manmade hill, next to a big rock. A circle of stones marks the spot for which we have been searching. Looking up, the depressions are easily identified. Fish Traps at last, handiwork from four or five centuries ago! About that time along this falling shoreline of the then salty Ancient Lake, eight to ten inch diameter rocks were rearranged in circular patterns forming the weirs. Outlets from these circles run toward the valley. The numerous Traps are placed in rows.

Archeologists believe the fish were caught when the wind blew water and fish up into the Fish Traps and Cahuilla nets were thrown over the rocks. Or perhaps bows and arrows or spears were used. No fishing hooks have been discovered indicating they did not fish from the shore like today's anglers. There are no well-worn trails to this place leading archeologists to believe that perhaps the fishing culture was present for only five to six years as it adapted to the ever-changing Colorado Desert's evaporating lake. Another controversial theory says that they were not fish traps at all but the remains of a large Pueblo and that the nearby petroglyphs are similar to Pueblo clan symbols found elsewhere in the West.

We now understand that the very difficulty in finding this unusual site could act as a protection for it. The damage already done by vandals and the encroaching agricultural fields threaten to further obliterate the Traps and petroglyphs.

We sit for a time in the hot sun wishing to feel the ancient water lapping at our feet. As we leave we wonder if the natives had shore

Ancient Fish Traps

lunches or smoked the fish and used it like jerky as we do on the trails today. One fish that was known to survive in brackish ocean water was the mullet. This saltwater fish is now rarely seen in the Salton Sea.

Travertine Rock

Back in the car, on the trail of more tufa and the Ancient Lake, we follow Avenue 66 to Highway 86. A mama coyote and three pups cross in front of the car. We take a right at Valerie Jeans Date Shop onto Highway 86. After 13 miles of driving with a brief stop at the Santa Rosa Date and Fruit shop in Oasis for a date shake, Travertine Rock looms up on the west side of the highway opposite Desert Shores Resort near the county line.

Last outpost of the Santa Rosa Mountains, Travertine Rock is covered by a hard crust of calcium carbonate deposited by receding water of the Ancient Lake. There are petroglyphs here but modern vandals have destroyed their secrets and from the highway the boulders of travertine have the look of the inner city. Sadly, we end our voyage here and make our way back along the land that once held an Ancient Sea.

Falling asleep that night, I saw the Ancient Lake, a dazzling blue gem. Our brief encounter with the Fish Traps of an ancient society on an Ancient Lake connects us for a time to the adaptive Cahuilla Indians whose lives center on nature and gives a glimpse into the tumultuous geology of the Valley.

Travel notes

The Fish Traps are located about 8 miles south of Indio and about 2 miles west of Valerie Jeans. Contact the Bureau of Land Management Palm Springs office for detailed directions: 760-833-7100. The Santa Rosa Date and Fruit shop and Valerie Jeans are no longer open. Valerie Jeans and Old King Solomon date palm are listed in the office of historic preservation of the California State Parks.

Easy Old-fashioned Raisin Sour Cream Pie

One hundred years ago adventurous picnickers to this area packed elaborate dinners. One such menu included fried chicken, potato salad, deviled eggs, home baked rolls, green tomato pickles, whipped cream cake, sour cream pie and coffee.

2 eggs
1 cup sugar
1 cup sour cream
1 cup raisins, chopped
¼ teaspoon nutmeg
⅛ teaspoon salt
1 tablespoon lemon juice
Purchased frozen Pillsbury pie crust for
a 9 inch covered pie

· Beat eggs slightly, add sugar, beat until light. Stir in remaining ingredients. Follow directions on pie crust and place one crust in bottom of pie pan. Pour filling into bottom crust. Trim and moisten edges of pastry. Cover with top crust, trim edges and crimp with fork or fingers. Pierce crust several times. Bake at 450 degrees 15 minutes. Bake 30 minutes longer at 350 degrees. If edges begin to brown too much cover with strips of foil.

Trail of the Desert Date

Driving tour of Shields, Jensens and Oasis
Date Gardens and Valerie Jeans Date Shop

&⬥ Banana Carob Pudding or Pie and Date Shake

Dates fortify us for our days wandering the desert as they have hu-
mankind from beyond recorded history. Where the date palm
grew, the ancient cultures of Chaldea, Assyria and Babylonia flourished. Considered the Tree of Life, it perhaps even grew in the Garden
of Eden. When King Tutankhamen's tomb was opened, dates were
found accompanying him into the afterlife. How did this treasured
morsel of the Sahara Valleys, of the Euphrates, Tigris and Nile come to
grow in the Colorado Desert?

Shields Date Garden

On the TRAIL OF THE DESERT DATE, we begin our wandering and tasting tour in Indio following Highway 111. Seated alone in the dark cool
Shields Romance Theater, Mom, Dad and I enjoy listening to E. F.
Shields expound on a continuous loop infomercial about dates. Back
in the days of two-lane roads and leisurely drives out into the country,
"The Romance and Sex Life of the Date" must have been quite an at-
traction here in Shield's: "Bit of Old Arabia in modern California." As
Mr. Shields explains on the fuzzy old movie, raising dates is a costly
operation. The land of the date grove itself now has become very valuable and the small groves remaining are squeezed between hotels, golf

Date Palm Sunset

photo credit: Evelyn McMillin

courses and Highway 111. Date trees are also coveted for landscaping golf courses and homes.

Date crystals and ice cream are whirled around in a blender to make a delicious date shake from an old-fashioned soda fountain for Dad and me. Outside, Mrs. Shield's rose garden and a small section of date grove invite a walk. Permanently mounted ladders on each tree intrigue us. These make it possible for date workers to tend the trees and shear the sharp thorns on new palm leaves. We now pursue our Trail to Jensens, just a few blocks away.

Jensens Date Shop

The widening of Highway 111 in the 1960s obliterated the original landmark building of Jensens Date Shop. The current small shop offers all varieties of dates and citrus fruits. Outside the shop, faded signs describe Coachella Valley geology and a garden features specimens of old citrus trees.

Continuing our Date Trail the next morning, we pass by the Indio fairgrounds. Here a Date Festival is a big event celebrated every February. On our way to Thermal, date palms laid out in symmetrical rows, trunks patterned by old leaf stalks, give a sense of going home; traveling along two-lane roads in a simpler time in the desert.

Nina Paul Shumway, a child of a date pioneer growing up along with the date industry, chronicled these years in Your Desert and Mine. Palms were introduced as an experiment to the hot interior valleys and Salton basin in the 1900s. The Department of Agriculture determined that the Coachella Valley would be ideal for cultivation of dates because of a climate so similar to the Sahara Desert.

The Arabs have a proverb that the palm to do well should have its feet in water and its head in the fire. The Colorado Desert fulfilled these conditions with its exceedingly hot summer temperatures and the slightly warm water from artesian wells that were so important in date irrigation.

Shumway's story continues with her father, William Paul, at the center of the great date experiment in the Coachella Valley. It was determined that growing trees from seed was too slow and did not produce consistent dates. Palm offshoots were the answer.

Subsequently, importers of offshoots from the Old World enticed speculative investing, pushing up costs and encouraging absentee proprietorship of date groves. This was recognized as detrimental to the date culture of the Valley. Shumway's father was successful in starting the first cooperative that benefitted the local Valley growers who contributed their agricultural expertise and lived right in the desert.

Now, almost a century later, the experiment has proven to be a monumental success. The Coachella Valley grows nearly all the dates for the United States. What is uncertain is whether in the future date palm groves will disappear from the desert altogether. Will all the Trees of Life be felled to plant houses and golf courses?

Oasis Date Garden

King David, a towering date palm, stands alone at the entrance to the Oasis Date Garden in Thermal. One large male tree produces enough pollen for his harem of 40–50 date producing female palms.

This working plantation, started in 1912 by Ben Laflin, is bustling with businessmen and women talking dates. Strolling around the store sampling varieties as if we are at a wine tasting, we nibble the rich caramel-colored Deglet Noor, the drier Khadrawi with soft pudding-like texture, the dark amber Barhi, the chewy medium sweet Zahidi, the honey-like Honey date and finish with our favorite, the royal Medjool.

In Morocco for many, many centuries, royalty and honored guests were the only ones allowed to savor the large, creamy, sweet delicacy called the Medjool. In the 1920s blight threatened the very existence of this mahogany date in their deserts. In an attempt to keep the trees from being wiped out, the Moroccan royal family sent eleven precious palms to another desert similar in climate, the Colorado in Southern California. Cultivated to perfection by the California growers, they are now the choice of the date connoisseur and we all have access to the "king of dates."

Too early for the morning tour of the 250-acre working date garden, I purchase Medjools and date sugar then slurp up another date shake as we walk the picnic area in the palm garden.

Valerie Jean Date Shop

Dust devils like whirling dervishes swirl on the road to Valerie Jean. This modest landmark, a 1928 pioneer date shop, is a large roadside stand at the corner of Highway 86 and Avenue 66. Inside the shop, a picture on the wall recalls the hardships of pioneer days when possessions were piled high in a wagon and a family traveled across the shifting sands of the desert on an old plank road.

Laden with Mexican-style green olives and organic sage honey, we leave the shop. No more date shakes for now but we have read that eating sweets can save your life in a desert climate. Sugar makes you thirsty and you need a strong thirst for the water necessary to keep hydrated in an arid climate.

Old King Solomon, another prolific male date palm, waves its fronds in a goodbye. Imported from Arabia in 1912, it produces enough pollen to father 3,600,000 dates yearly.

The art of growing dates in the Coachella Valley continues an ancient practice and we can only hope in years to come King Solomon and King David or their offshoots will still be commanding respect in the Colorado Desert.

Travel notes

Shield's Date Garden is at 80-225 Highway 111 in Indio. They are
open daily 9 a.m. -5 p.m. daily except holidays. Information: www.
shieldsdategarden.com or 760-347-0996. Jensens Date and Citrus
Garden and Valerie Jeans in Thermal are no longer open for business.
Valerie Jeans and Old King Solomon date palm are listed in the office
of historic preservation of the California State Parks. From Indio
continuing on Highway 111, pass Coachella. The Oasis Date Gardens
in Thermal are at 59-111 Highway 111. Open daily. Call for holiday
hours. Information: www.oasisdategardens.com or 760-399-5665 or
800-827-8017. There are picnic tables in an oasis setting.

In Indio, the Coachella Valley History Museum is off Highway 111
at 82-616 Miles Avenue. The museum grounds contain the Smiley-
Tyler House, a 1909 schoolhouse, Date Museum and variety of
gardens. Admission fee: nominal. Open 10 a.m.-4 p.m. Thursday–
Saturday, 1p.m.–4 p.m. Sunday. Closed July and August. Information:
www.coachellavalleymuseum.org or 760-342-6651

Banana Carob Pudding or Pie

Recipe provided by Michael Miller, certified Gourmet Raw Food
Chef and Instructor from Living Light Culinary Institute. He can
be reached at www.lindampyle.com. This light and delicious pie
or pudding is gluten and dairy free and requires no baking.
Tip: Bananas that are brown and speckled are ripe and nutritious.
They are usually sold at a cheaper price and can be frozen for future
use.

Pudding or Pie Filling
4 ripe medium-size ripe bananas
3 small avocados, pitted
1 packed cup of pitted Medjool dates
4 tablespoons raw or toasted carob powder (health food store)

· Cut avocados in half, remove pits and scoop out flesh. Blend with
bananas, dates and carob powder in a food processor until in a
creamy frosting-like consistency. (Crust recipe following page.)

Crust for Banana Carob Pie

1 cup almonds
1 cup walnuts
1 packed cup of pitted Medjool dates

· Process nuts pulsing in a food processor until they are in a fine ground texture. Add dates and process until mixture begins to form a ball. Grease a 9 inch pie pan with olive oil. Press crust into bottom. Pour in filling. Freeze for several hours until set. Serve at refrigerator temperature. Freeze unused portions.

Frozen Yogurt Date Shake

This nonfat delicious shake is inspired by Mrs. Shield's recipe using their date crystals.

1½ cups partially frozen nonfat milk
1½ cups frozen vanilla yogurt
½ cup date crystals
¼ cup nonfat milk

· Mix date crystals with ¼ cup milk and refrigerate for several hours. Partially freeze 1½ cups nonfat milk. In a blender whirl all ingredients together and pour into tall shake glasses. Serves 2–3.

Trail of a Spectacular Canyon
and an Accidental Sea

Hiking Ladder and Painted Canyon and visiting the Salton Sea

ઢ **Walnut Carob Fudge Brownies**

O n our TRAIL OF A SPECTACULAR CANYON we parked next to a smoldering campfire at the end of Painted Canyon Road. We walked down Painted Canyon less than one half mile to the place where we would slip into the sedimentary rock. This canyon is located in the Mecca Hills which run along the San Andreas Fault. Here, ancient seabed rocks were once forced up into mountains which were eroded and worn down by wind and rain then pushed up once again.

The sandstone and conglomerates have been crushed and melded together by earthquake action. The sun ignites Technicolor hues of travertine green, ash gray, gold and russet red. When oxidized, the iron in the shale walls combined with other minerals changes color resulting in the purples, reds, oranges and yellows we see in this ravine.

Ladder Canyon

I put my foot on the first rung of the aluminum ladder, and climbed down into the sandstone just off the main wash marked by a sign opposite a jumble of fallen rocks. Was this ladder placed by some Bureau of Land Management worker, some Boy Scout, some local hiker? I didn't know but I thanked them. T.M. and I climbed like children down into the womb of the ravine cut into the sedimentary rock. I was light in my boots flying down the ladder that took me inside a magic pink sand castle.

When we reached the next ladder, lickety-split, we repeated the descent, down, down, down, to where I declared myself a lucky human as we slipped into the slots getting tighter and tighter. Smiling was easy, around the next bend, down one more boulder, up one more ladder and then the slow climb out to the ridge high above the main canyon. It was like, going back in time, back in ages, back beyond, back to childhood, dangerous curves, and steep stairs. Didn't mother waiting in the car say don't run with sharp scissors, don't wander in far-off places where one might ride the floodwaters sweeping us down to the Salton Sea on a ride of boulders and dirt and whatnot? Hiking up the wash we could see the effect of powerful flash floods cutting through the earth in deep swathes. The cliffs held fossils and stones in suspension. Buckskin-colored sandstone crumbled in my fingers. Just a few initials were carved into the ancient face.

Too soon it seemed, we were spit out onto a high ridge-back and then down into the main Painted Canyon. This was more than a canyon, it was an immense geological wonder created by faulting, wind and weather. I had become younger. My hands gripped the trekking poles, my ears heard the gleeful echoes of the other kids in front of me, hey, weren't we all kids out here, in this playground of geological time, rock of ages.

Polite conversation seemed inappropriate here in the grandeur. We should have been rebel yelling, whooping it up, whistling but we were quiet in reverence for the great wonder and striking features crafted by water. How small we were, how insignificant little us, on the ladders made of aluminum, in leather boots, wearing packs, slogging up the canyon past palo verde and iron wood trees, past metamorphic rock changed by heat and pressure. Who were we in this desert playground time but small creatures on two legs, just wanting a taste of the eternal creation of earth, so near the faults, so near the squeezing pressure, so near the powerful forces that create beauty. We go to be reborn ourselves, newly evolved creatures fresh from the depths of Ladder Canyon, to climb down the final ladder over the dry waterfall down to where our car was parked, where the campfire still smoldered. Mom snapped a picture of me standing like an icon in a rocky niche.

Thoughts of sabotaging our itinerary to spend the whole day here evaporate as our ambitious plans head us toward the largest lake in California. The mysterious blue Salton Sea glistens like pewter against the low mountains rising above the west shore as we leave the Painted Canyon. We cross back over the Canal bringing the Colorado River water to the Imperial and Coachella Valleys making possible the vast agricultural pursuits in what is now one of the most productive farming areas on earth. The desert has given up 600,000 acres to this enterprise.

Salton Sea

Arriving at this Sea within the desert was once more popular than a trip to Yosemite. Today, it is quiet and the picnic tables of the campgrounds empty. A smoky blue haze settles over the San Jacinto Mountains in the distance. The water is dotted with squawking gulls. The smell of dried fish is in the cool breeze off the lake. At first, it assaults the nose but one soon forgives its earthy smell.

This former playland for many is now under critical environmental strain. As a link in the Pacific migratory flyway, it substitutes for the lost wetlands of the Los Angeles basin. Due to agricultural run off and polluted sewage from Mexico, it is increasingly contaminated and subject to high levels of salt. People still come but no longer in droves. The birds who do and the fish in the lake are dying at an unbelievable rate from unknown causes. The Sea is both a sanctuary and a hazard.

At the Salton Sea Recreational Area Visitor Center we learn how this sea was formed by mistake. The Salton Sea today is a lesser reincarnation of the Ancient Lake Cahuilla. The sea reformed by accident in 1905 and 1906 when the Colorado River once again partially filled the depression left by the Ancient Lake. The river poured into the valley for two years, this time as a result of spring floods and failed gates on the canal designed to bring water to the valley. Surrounding homes, farms and the New Liverpool Salt Company that was employed in collecting salt left by the ancient gulf and evaporated lakes were destroyed. When the gap was finally closed, a lake 45 miles long and 17 miles wide with a surface 195 feet below sea level remained. Shriveling over time, the lake today is 35 miles long, 15 miles wide and 228 feet below sea level.

Salton Sea Picnic

Leaving the Visitor center to walk along the shore, we are astonished by the crunch under our feet and discover our shoes are treading upon uncrushed pearly pink shells, ancient shells not yet ground into sand.

We have a light snack in the shade of a ramada and reflect upon the silvery, salty, shallow lake.

San Andreas Fault

Cataclysmic changes in the earth and sea are near. We are sinking in the Salton Sink, that seam along the San Andreas fault where the Pacific and Continental plates continue to grind into each other; the Sink is subsiding at a rate of about 2.5 inches a year. If I were to go with it, at my height of 5 feet, I'd be underground in 24 years. The bedrock of the original surface is buried 4 miles below us. We almost hear the creak and groan of the earth's surface metamorphosing. Proximity to the San Andreas Fault may give some the jitters but it has helped create the enigmatic incomparable landscape of Southern California.

Across the lake, silent shapes loom spectrally on the horizon. Could a pearl-seeking Spanish galleon have reached the ancient inland sea by sailing up the Colorado River and have been covered by shifting sands? There is such a story.

The story related by the men who walked into Guaymas, Mexico, was that their ship's Captain Iturbe had led an expedition farther and farther into the Sea of Cortez until he was in the area of the Colorado Delta. His prize was to be huge pearls supposedly produced by giant mollusks. When attempting to return with some of these pearls, a change in the geography of the area, thought to have been caused by an earthquake, prevented them from sailing out; they abandoned the ship and trudged all the way to Guaymas, Mexico. Subsequently, a mast and a spar were said to have been seen in the sand. The legend may be explained as a desert mirage with a pearly sheen or it may be true.

Another ghost story tells of strange sounds coming from Superstition Mountain across the water. Indians avoided it, fearing the eerie noises. Prisoners held at a nearby camp complained about disturbing sounds. A ghostly presence or sounds from the rock that is riddled with caves under the sand covering the mountain?

Ironwood Nature Trail

At the nearby Ironwood Nature Trail, we leave Dad in the shade of a feathery tamarisk tree and walk the crunchy salt pan through tall marsh grass. We find this very low section of the desert very high in salt and alkali. The goldenbush and jagged leafed desert holly that brushes our legs must have a high tolerance for salt.

The Whitewater, Alamo and New Rivers feed the Salton Sea, saltier than the ocean. The runoff water from many streams and irrigation canals is low in salinity but nevertheless adds millions of tons of salt to the lake each year. Evaporation leaves the salt and minerals behind. Eventually, the sea may become too saline even for fish.

Once traded for gold, salt is a mysterious necessity. Man needs common salt to maintain the balance of his own internal sea. It is more important to life and movement than the gold sought here in the mountains. Animals and man were once tied to the salt lick. Learning to preserve with salt made poor food more palatable and transportable and in the long run made civilization possible.

Before the flooding of the lake in 1905 and 1906, vast deposits of very pure salt were mined here by the New Liverpool Salt Company. The collection of salt was an unusual process. Cahuilla Indians plowed the salt into enormous piles. Conveyed by a tram railway, it was transported to the New Liverpool Company where Japanese and Indians ground, sacked and shipped it. This operation came to an abrupt end when the floods occurred.

The salt pan trail moves away from the water and as Mom departs to go back, I show her a possible arrowhead. We surmise it may have been made from molten magma pushed up to the surface of the fractured thin earth crust along the Salton Trough during the time of earthquakes and volcanoes. Obsidian Butte and Mullet Island on the southeast side of the Sea were created from this process as well as hot springs and mud pots. When the lake was dry, Cahuilla Indians broke off volcanic glass chips for knives and arrow points.

Having greatly underestimated the time it would take to drive even one-half the way around the 110 miles of shoreline means that the Salton Sea National Wildlife Refuge and Obsidian Butte will have to wait.

And so we had walked amid the splendor of a Canyon and looked into the shallow water of the Salton Sea and seen her former lives. We turned the car around and headed toward Thermal. I was in need of an Oasis Date Garden date shake.

Travel notes

To reach Painted Canyon take I-10 east 6.5 miles from Indio to 86S expressway. Go 10.5 miles south to 62nd Avenue. Turn left and go 2.3 miles. Turn right on Johnson Street. Go 2 miles to 66th Street. Turn left and proceed 5.1 miles to Painted Canyon Road. This road may require a high clearance vehicle depending on conditions. Go left on the unpaved road to its end and park at the junction of the canyons at the end of the road.

To hike Ladder Canyon proceed into upper Painted Canyon for .4 mile. Look for the trail marker for Ladder Canyon on your right. (It is possible it will not be there.) Look up on your left and climb up the fallen boulders to a series of aluminum ladders that ascend and descend into the ravine carved out of the sedimentary rock. At .8 mile (from the parking area) take the right fork and at 1.1 miles you will top out on a ridge. At the top go left and at 1.35 miles continue straight on the ridge. At 2 miles you will be above a wash. Head down into the wash of Painted Canyon. Go right and slog downhill. Climb down one more ladder over a dry waterfall. This moderate to strenuous (due to ladders and quick ascent) 4.3 mile hike has 1,500 feet elevation change and takes about 2.5 hours.

To reach the Salton Sea take I-10 east approximately 6.5 miles from Indio to the 86S expressway 12.6 miles to 66th Avenue east. Go .8 mile to Highway 111. Turn right and proceed 10.8 miles. Park Headquarters for the Salton Sea State Recreation area will be on your right.

Information: www.seaanddesert.com The Ironwood Nature Trail is a flat loop that starts at the visitor center campground and goes south down the beach. Be sure and check out the 15 minute video on the Sea. Learn why some scientists have called the Salton Sea, "California's crown jewel of avian biodiversity." Varner Harbor now has a launch area for kayaks.

Oasis Date Garden information: see page 143.

Recipe provided by Michael Miller, certified Gourmet Raw Food Chef and Instructor from Living Light Culinary Institute. He can be reached at www.lindampyle.com. *Raw food is a diet that is plant-based, consisting of fresh, ripe fruit, vegetables, nuts, seeds and sprouted grains. This easy to make brownie is gluten and dairy free and contains no refined sugar.

Walnut Carob Fudge Brownies

7 pitted Medjool dates
2 ½ cups walnuts
½ cup raisins
6 tablespoons carob powder (from health food store)
½ teaspoon ground Himalayan salt

· Process walnuts in a food processor into crumbled mixture. Add the rest of the ingredients except raisins and ½ cup of walnuts reserved. Add 3 tablespoons water to mixture and process into dough ball. Mix in by hand the raisins and ½ cup rough chopped walnuts. Press into an 8x8 inch baking pan. Freeze. To serve cut into squares. Keep unused portions frozen.

Trail of a Larger than Life
World War II Soldier

*General Patton Memorial Museum at Chiriaco Summit
and Desert Flight Museum in Palm Springs*

ॐ Forties Tuna and Blueberry Salad

I *was with Patton.*

This statement used by World War II veterans in his divisions was unique in the American Army as the cult of personality was only rarely seen. Only a singular person could inspire such remarks whether they reflected admiration or dislike. Flamboyant, colorful, hated and loved but always dedicated to his men and country, he cut a large figure in the winning of World War II.

Taking the scenic route along Highway 111 south, we turn east through the town of Mecca on Avenue 66 and cross the Coachella canal. Speeding along Box Canyon Road (Highway 195) on the right are the Orocopia Mountains, a magnet for miners when gold was found in 1885. Whizzing by twisted, tortured trees interspersed with greening smoke trees in a Sahara desert setting, we are soon paralleling Highway 10 and a rugged undeveloped land perfect for desert training in World War II.

General Patton Museum

On the TRAIL OF A LARGER THAN LIFE WORLD WAR II SOLDIER at the General Patton Museum, we walk among some of the camouflaged mechanical behemoth tanks of an era forever etched into the

General Patton Museum

American psyche. When General George Smith Patton Jr., commander of the Army's First (I) Corps established a center for desert warfare training in March of 1942 in this land of: "sand, choking dust and rattlesnakes," he chose well. The men who trained here went on to succeed in the battles for North Africa and Europe.

Patton made Camp Young his headquarters and the Desert Training Center soon was expanded to 350 miles wide and 250 miles deep to include ten more camps, massive tent cities. Nearly one million soldiers trained in this harsh environment.

Many sacrifices were being made at that time by the general public in the pursuit of victory over the German Nazis. One of these may be said to be the sacrifice of the pristine peace of this desert. This home of the ocotillo, creosote, chuckwalla and coyote became the home of fire-breathing juggernauts and men dedicating their lives to obliterating a hated enemy. Aboriginal sites bombed, canyons and mesas overrun by jeeps and tanks, the desert was scarred forever.

War memorabilia, uniforms and captured Nazi flags line the walls inside the cool museum. We sit in the dark watching a video about General Patton. The toughness, profanity and braggadocio for which he became so well-known were consciously cultivated by him as was the war-face so striking in his pictures. The use of a "war persona" he felt gave his men a battle disguise to overcome any fear of death.

Such was the man who took command here and lived among the Palm Springites for only four months. He turned the swank El Mirador Hotel into a hospital treating veterans from battlefields all over the world. The area now known as Palm Desert was the site of his tank repair depot and the La Quinta resort grounds were taken over by the Army Tank and Army Air Corps.

And such was the man who led his men into the largest amphibious operation ever attempted in the surf of Morocco, North Africa. After advancing with much loss of life in the sea due to inexperienced landing craft sailors and bad weather conditions, negotiations and the surrender of the Vichy French left Patton in command of Casa Blanca. Further activity joined with the British against the German forces in Tunisia was also successful. The decision to conquer Sicily by the Allied troop leaders found Patton in charge of the Seventh American Army.

Unfortunate and career changing events now unfolded. Patton did the unthinkable and slapped soldiers in sick bay for what he though was cowardice. Then, in another incident, he ranted and raved at a shell-shocked soldier and physically assaulted him. These vicious attacks put General Eisenhower under such pressure when word leaked out that he ordered Patton to make a public apology. General Omar Bradley, of lesser rank, was given the job of commanding the American 1st Army in the invasion of Western Europe. Patton survived the incident only by the esteem Eisenhower had for his valuable assets to the war effort.

His belief that war could be won by "self confidence, speed and audacity" stood him in good stead in Europe after D. Day in the battle for Germany when the enemy was forced back into Germany itself. The essential crossings of the Rhine so important in the Allies advance found Patton's troops eventually eliminating the German 7th and 1st Armies.

Outside in the heat of Camp Young, we stop to touch the cold silent tanks that helped create peace. The camps were closed and abandoned in '44 to the mercies of the desert leaving only remnants of life at the camps: white rocks that once lined the roads, stone altars and rock insignias of some of the camps. Preserving and interpreting the camps has been left to the Bureau of Land Management.

During a break for iced tea at the old-fashioned Chiriaco Café next door, we wonder what it would be like to be entombed in the tanks that helped win World War II as we head for other fighting machines at the Palm Springs Air Museum. We whisk from the Patton Museum towards Palm Springs along Highway 10 to the Palm Springs Air Museum continuing a nostalgic World War II history trail for Mom and Dad.

Palm Springs Air Museum

Once sabre-toothed tigers and wild cats roamed this desert floor. We are not on their trail today but seek to find the Grumman Wildcat, Hellcat, Tigercat and Bearcat preserved here.

We enter a large hangar smelling of oil, showcasing propeller-driven World War II aircraft in flying condition. Included in the museum is one of the world's largest collections of fighting World War II airplanes, legendary fighters and bombers that helped win World War II. We spot an A-26 fighter bomber model like the one Dad worked on as an aeronautical engineer for Douglas Aircraft in Long Beach, California in the days when the city was under lights out, camouflaged conditions. Even President Bush could visit the plane he flew here, as could many other veterans who participated in World War II.

Battles fought on the land and battles fought in the air are commemorated here in the desert at the Palm Springs Air Museum and General Patton Museum. "History through the eyes of those who were there."

Travel notes

The General Patton Museum is located 30 miles east of Indio at the Chiriaco Summit exit on Interstate 10. Follow the signs. Open daily 9:30 am –4:30 p.m. Closed Christmas and Thanksgiving. Admission fees: adults, $5.00, seniors $4.50, children 7-12 $1. Information: www.generalpattonmuseum.com or 760-227-3483

An alternate scenic route can be taken along Highway 111 south from Palm Desert turning east through the town of Mecca on Avenue 66, crossing over the Coachella canal, then following Box Canyon Road, Highway 195, to Interstate 10. Exit Chiriaco Summit and follow the signs.

The Air Museum is located near the Palm Springs Regional Airport, 745 North Gene Autry Trail. Open daily 10 a.m.–5 p.m. Closed Thanksgiving and Christmas Day. Admission fees: adults $14.00, seniors, retired military and youth 13-17 $12.00, children 6-12 $7.00. Information: 760-778-6262 or www.palmspringsairmuseum.org

Forties Blueberry Tuna Salad

¼ pound small pasta shells, cooked
One 12 ounce can water packed tuna
¼ cup sliced black or green olives
½ cup celery, diced
½ cup red onion, diced
¼ cup red pepper, diced
2 teaspoons dried dill
¼–½ cup mayonnaise
¼ cup blueberries

· Mix ingredients together. Refrigerate for several hours. Add salt and pepper to taste. Sprinkle blueberries on top of salad and serve with quartered hard-boiled eggs and tomatoes. Serves 4–5.

Trail of the Bradshaw
Stage Line at Dos Palmas

*Short walk to oasis along San Andreas and El Alamo Trail
and challenging hike to Dos Palmas Preserve*

ε♣ New Fangled Slumgullion

Bleak, chocolate-colored escarpments loom over the sun-blistered desert floor like sentinels. Clouds of dust stirred up by wooden wheels and pounding hooves signal an approaching stagecoach. Dressed in long black duster and leather hat, a "knight of the silk" cracks his whip.

Parched passengers, obsessed with the need for water having endured long waterless miles and terrible alkali water, strain to see two green fan palm trees like exclamation points on the horizon marking an oasis. Dos Palmas Stagecoach Station is now in sight; a flat-roofed structure thatched with overhanging palm fronds. Arriving passengers and animals could now drink their fill of water. Travelers would relax in the grass and bathe in the warm pool in this utter isolation and reclaim their sanity.

What makes this torturous mode of travel in the Old West seem so romantic and exciting to us that we ended up in the Colorado Desert on the TRAIL OF THE BRADSHAW STAGE LINE AT DOS PALMAS? Maybe we are as entranced with this past method of travel as Easterners were in the 1860s reading about "seeing the elephant" in the Far West. This common expression of the time meant either to venture out into new

Road to Dos Palmas

territory with high hopes or to return home having seen more than enough disappointment.

Is this why I had jumped from the car against the wishes of the "threshold guardian?" I now realized the historic Dos Palmas was not the small San Andreas Oasis we had just hiked near the parking area but an unknown distance and location down a gated road posted, "ONLY WALKING."

Dos Palmas

Walking furiously down the dirt road toward the unknown, I pondered the answer. Did I half hope that some remnant of the Dos Palmas stage station days would still remain? Was I perhaps chasing handsome William D. Bradshaw himself who forged the Bradshaw Trail? I longed for a stagecoach to pull up, open the door and let me join the passengers.

A stagecoach and driver of a different sort does arrive in a strange way for me; the coach is not made of varnished live oak but of metal and steel. A large green vehicle with flat bed and bulldozer on top, a Bureau of Land Management truck comes to a stop courteously not wishing to pelt me with gravel. A bearded knight steps down from his cab and in answer to my question: "Where is Dos Palmas?" invites me to step up on the flat bed to scan the horizon for the faraway palms. Making sure my water bottle is full, he disappears down the undulating road, agreeing to tell Mom and Dad that I am on the right path. Following a sign and an arrow, I leave the road on a diagonal path toward the green oasis, passing ponds reflecting an aquamarine sky.

The BLM and Nature Conservancy manage the 30,000-acre oasis preserve I walk, a significant Sonoran desert wetland habitat nestled on the floor below the Orocopia and Chocolate Mountains. Abundant fresh water from a perennial flow along earthquake faults supports the fan palms, avian and aquatic life including the rare Yuma clapper rail and endangered desert pupfish. Dos Palmas, purchased by the Nature Conservancy in 1989, includes 14,000 acres with old fishponds. On the Pacific flyway between the Colorado and the Mohave Deserts, the Preserve provides an essential habitat for millions of resident and visiting migratory birds. This makes it one of the best birding areas in the entire Southwest. I spot only one bird near the edge of a pond, my lone companion on the trail.

Native Americans used the Dos Palmas Spring as a major stopping point for travel. When gold was discovered in La Paz, (near present day Ehrenberg, Arizona across the Colorado River) in 1862, William D. Bradshaw was chosen to find the best route to the mines from the pueblo of Los Angeles.

It is said this charming Southern gentleman had a gift for speaking dialects. Perhaps this is why when he had a fortuitous meeting with Chief Cabezon and a visiting Maricopa Indian from Arizona, they drew Bradshaw a map of the ancient trade route across the desert and important water holes; information which had never been shared with Anglos.

The newspaper in Los Angeles printed Bradshaw's description of the route helping to publicize this trail, which ran through the Salt Creek wash between the Orocopia and Chocolate Mountains to the Colorado River. Dos Palmas was then used as a stage stop along the water-starved Bradshaw Trail. The sight of the oasis, Dos Palmas, when it was a "home station" must have been welcome indeed.

The "home station" provided a place to sleep and food usually of questionable quality. Whips or Jehus, as these fleet drivers were called, switched here to continue the trip on to Los Angeles. When it was only a "swing station" passengers got a less satisfying stop, maybe a mid-day meal. Replacing the tired team with fresh livestock was the main objective.

I keep my eye on the Oasis that seems close but it is as if I am running in place in a dream. This is a landscape where the imagination can run wild. The palms never seem to be in reach, only patches of white alkali and thickets of gray mesquite. I keep looking back, keenly concerned not to lose my sense of direction back to the road, and rush forward into the past.

Dos Palmas played a major role along the trail and became a junction for roads leading to mines in the desert and mountains. A serious blow was dealt to stage travel in 1878, when the Southern Pacific Railroad opened lines to San Bernardino making travel in this unforgiving stretch of desert less hazardous.

The Bradshaw Trail, though used less by travelers, remained in service throughout the mining era of the turn of the century. An ore mill built at Dos Palmas serviced the miners working the Orocopia Mountains. Desert prospectors found rejuvenation in the spring for themselves and their trustworthy pack burros.

Tales of missing gold always pique keen interest in amateur prospectors. One such story figures in Dos Palmas history. A road agent held up the stage from La Paz, murdering the driver, getting away with the "treasure box," the stagecoach strong box filled with gold. Confident enough to rob the stage but arrogant to the extreme, the bandit bought a round of drinks for passengers at the bar at Dos Palmas. The bandit becoming suspicious that the sheriff had been notified tried to escape but was killed. Because very little gold was found on his body, the story circulated that he had buried the rest of his booty somewhere along the trail. Many searches have been made but the treasure is always undetected and only the desert sands know the truth.

The Dos Palmas property changed hands many times until 1939 when it was operated as a guest ranch. In World War II, General Patton as part of his Desert Army Training Center used the land. The series of mirage-imitating pools of water remain from the days when Dos Palmas was more recently a commercial fish farm.

In the distance, hundreds of palms instead of the original two proliferate, screening the heart of Dos Palmas Oasis from me. I feel the exhilaration of being alone in a wild place that now belongs only to the palms. Estimating it would take another hour or two of exploring, I think of Mom and Dad sweltering in a hot car waiting behind the gate. Abandoning my attempt to reach the phantom station and its mysteries, I stop chasing the past and race back to the car. With the scent of mesquite in the cool wind behind me, retreating in defeat, I realize I have found not the romance of stage days but the loneliness, the separation and the uncertainty of the stage traveler in a hostile environment.

At the end of my run and at the car I am greeted with: "You look hot as a beetle!" Just starting to get irritated and worried about my long absence, Mom says the earlier morning exploration of the San Andreas Oasis was certainly an easier task! But I had seen the "elephant" and they had not.

Before my trek to Dos Palmas, we had walked the San Andreas and El Alamo Trail. Here our footprints mingled with the prints of a roadrunner, a coyote and a little snake that had crossed the rock-edged path to the spring ahead earlier. Entering into the palm-protected grotto, we meandered through a small oasis. When we left our tracks were soon brushed away by the wind but we took away the remembrance of unseen life and things past.

Travel notes

Take I-10 east approximately 6.5 miles from Indio to the 86S express-way 12.6 miles to 66th Avenue east. Go .8 mile to Highway 111. Turn right and proceed 10.8 miles. Park Headquarters for the Salton Sea State Recreation area will be on your right. Turn left opposite the Park onto Parkside Drive. Take Parkside to its end, about 2 miles, and turn right on Desert Aire and proceed to its end. Turn left onto the unsigned dirt road. Take the next left fork and follow the signs to Dos Palmas. There is parking near the San Andreas Trail. There is a 1.5 mile loop trail through the San Andreas Palms near the parking area.

Dos Palmas is reached on foot only. Allow 2-3 hours on a cool day to hike out and back from the historic rancho, palm oasis and pools.

In 1974, Riverside County officially named the road from Dos Palmas east to Ludy Boulevard in Palo Verde Valley, the Bradshaw Trail. Nothing remains of the Dos Palmas stage station.

New Fangled Slumgullion

Western frontier slumgullion was a meat and vegetable stew unflatteringly named for the mud that comes out of the downhill end of a sluice, a trough used for washing gold-bearing dirt in a placer mine. Possibly it was served at the home station at Dos Palmas. Perhaps by newspaper, this recipe was circulated in the Midwest and my Grandmother made her own version that incorporated macaroni.

1 pound lean ground turkey or hamburger
1 tablespoon oil
1 medium onion, chopped
1 clove garlic, minced
1 stalk celery, diced
¼ red or green pepper, diced (if desired)
One 28 ounce can diced tomatoes
¼ teaspoon sugar
1/3 pound small elbow macaroni
1 cup water
Sea salt
Freshly ground pepper

- Heat oil over medium heat in heavy skillet. Sauté meat until no longer pink. Add onion, celery, garlic and red or green pepper and continue cooking until onion is opaque. Add tomato, sugar, salt and pepper. Cook 20 minutes more. Add 1 cup water and uncooked macaroni. Cook 20 more minutes until macaroni is tender. Serves 5–6.

Trail of the Wind

Wind Farm Tour

❧ Date Pecan Cheesecake

The prevailing west wind, the scourer of the desert and scourge of the sun seeker, led us on our TRAIL OF THE WIND to the San Gorgonio Pass northwest of Palm Springs. We left the paved surface road and turned up a dirt road and began to climb. Our tour guide, Craig, had picked us up at our hotel for the 90 minute tour. We were on BLM, short for Bureau of Land Management, leased land in a forest of thousands of three story giants that dominated the landscape and dazzled the eye with spinning white blades.

He brought the Hummer to a stop at a high plateau spot, turned and looked at us. "Hold onto your hats," he said. He opened his door, got out, shut the door and headed toward the cliff edge.

Ingleside Inn

We were staying for the weekend at the famous Ingleside Inn with friends from San Francisco. It had all the charm and rat pack history we had expected but we were delighted to find the staff had a friendly, accommodating attitude and good sense of humor like the owner of the Inn, Mel Haber. T.M. had been entertaining us at breakfast by reading out loud Mel's book called *Bedtime Stories of the Legendary Ingleside Inn*, about Sir John Beech, the once touted toast of Palm Springs society owning mansions around the world and 2 Rolls Royces, and a turquoise mine, or so he said. Our large rooms fronted the porch where breakfast was served under the lovely old

Wind Farm Tour

vines and best of all we were nestled close to the San Jacinto Mountain. It was a September afternoon without a wisp of air moving. This was a stark contrast to what we were about to experience outside the Hummer.

Wind Farm Tour

We opened the back doors, stepped out of the vehicle into the crazy bluster then yanked the doors closed behind us. We caught up to our guide walking into wind that impeded our progress. He had rushed on ahead of us and had now leaned over a cliff with his arms held out like a sky diver. He stepped back from the edge. He held a wind anemometer in his hand and told us a 35 knot wind (that's 40.3 mph) held his body upright and suspended. That's enough to break twigs off trees if there were any out here. I peered over the edge and wow, I looked down hundreds of feet. "What is that down there?" I said. I felt giddy like a school kid on a field trip. Didn't we all love that day we got out of regular classroom and got on a yellow bus with our school chums to go learn something new? It was exciting like that. Craig was our fun teacher whose enthusiasm for his energy subject inspired us. Craig had to yell over the wind to answer my question. "That's the Whitewater River down there. And there's where the Colorado River water is being discharged into the valley aquifer." From this high point out to our east we could see the holding ponds. He had already shown us earlier the complex of buildings which were the monitoring stations for the wind companies.

The hot wind heated up my plastic contact lenses. I squinted, held onto my hat which had nearly turned inside out, gave up on taking a photo and let the wind rip around the resistance of my body unlike the smooth white towers of the windmills. The wind blew up my skirt. It tore at my hat strings and brim. It tore at my shirt and billowed out my sleeves. The gusts nearly blew me off my feet. Yet, I loved this wind. It was renewable energy. Predictable wind patterns occur in the Pass where cool dense air flows inland from the coast as the hot air over the Coachella Valley rises. The V of the soaring San Gorgonio and the high San Jacinto Mountains creates a wind tunnel. Craig told us the mills are located here in the pass because the wind blows a predictable 12 mph or more for 280 days a year. But when the wind accelerates to more than 55 mph (that's enough to uproot a tree) the mills have to shut down. He showed us how the new turbines were getting taller, bigger, and more efficient. And that the manufacturing of parts for the mills had created many jobs in America. Now that's good news. I had a cousin who was working many hours doing the back breaking work of installing turbine towers in Iowa.

We collected our artist friend who was busy photographing the unique visual images and piled back in the vehicle. Craig drove us to another location where we got out and stood under the turbines. With our heads craned back and eyes turned up, the landscape was strange, haunted, yet beautiful in some odd sculptural way. We could hear the whoosh of the blades over our heads. Some windmill blades remained stationary while others spun like Tour de France bike wheels. The wind caught the fiberglass blades which caused them to turn and spin the rotor of the generator to which they were attached.

"Cool isn't it?" Craig said.

We nodded, smiled, and got back in the vehicle to drive by a sort of graveyard for dinosaur lattice-type windmills laid on their sides, fallen like chopped trees. Ever wonder what happens to old windmills when they die? It's churn, burn and abandon baby, right where they fall. Can you believe that?

Back on the paved road on our way back to the Inn, Craig

condensed other downsides of these farms as bird kills and strobe-like sunset flicker from the long shadows of blades for nearby Desert Hot Springs. There had been some wind sabotage between competing companies which had been amicably settled, there were nixed plans to advertise all over the white blades and there was a bat kill problem solved by drilling a hole in the blade tips. And of course the biggest issue of all was the waning and waxing tax incentives.

Our guide delivered us back to the calm, Ingleside Inn. We thanked Craig for the professional, first class tour and he drove off. Our friends disappeared into their rooms for an afternoon nap. T.M. and I sat down by the pool. The air was languid and still. T.M. began again reading out loud about Sir John wearing a crown and red cape into the Melvyn's Restaurant dining room one night. People were flocking to the Inn to get a glimpse of him.

Then, boom, like a curtain had dropped, the pool was in complete shade. The sun had set behind the mountains and it was time for dinner.

Another great thing about the Inn was we could walk downtown. While dining at the Johannes Restaurant, T.M. told our friends about Sir John and how he had finally been busted by the Palm Springs police, exposed as a house painter from Detroit with a long criminal rap sheet. But he had so captured the heart of the community he was still thought of with some degree of fondness. He had studied the ways of the rich and had ingratiated himself with locals who wanted to believe in his fairy tale. The meal was delicious, the service good and the atmosphere lively.

That night I closed my eyes and listened to the hum of the air conditioner. I saw the tall smooth towers lifting those pinwheel shapes three stories in the air. I saw them lined up in even lines like headstones in a military cemetery. I saw eyesores on the land. I saw beauty in the symmetry of the windmill towers. I saw the new fed springs of energy collection demanded by our energy consumption and desire for renewable resources.

The next morning there was the festive Sunday Champagne brunch at Melvyn's. We chatted and joked with the staff who had been with the Inn for decades. Then we packed up to head for the airport to drop off our friends. As we drove out the driveway we passed Mr. Haber arriving. I already missed the closeness of the mountain, the humor of the owner and the peace of this historic inn and we were already making plans to return. What a fun weekend and we had a much better understanding of wind power.

Travel notes

Elite Land Tours 90 minute excursion - 4 or more guests $49pp / 3 guests $69pp / 2 guests $79pp. Information: www.elitelandtours.com or 760-318-1200 or 800-514-4866. Bring sunglasses, sunscreen and water.

The Ingleside Inn is at 200 West Ramon Road at Belardo Road. Information: www.inglesideinn.com or 760-325-0046

The Johannes Restaurant is at 196 S. Indian Canyon Dr. Information: 760-778-0017.

Recipe provided by Michael Miller, certified Gourmet Raw Food Chef and Instructor from Living Light Culinary Institute. He can be reached at www.lindampyle.com.

*Raw food is a diet that is plant-based, consisting of fresh, ripe fruit, vegetables, nuts, seeds and sprouted grains. This cheesecake has no refined sugar or dairy and is gluten free. It is light and delicious.

Date Pecan Cheesecake

Crust
2 cups pecans
8 large pitted Medjool dates

Cheesecake
3 cups raw cashews (soaked overnight)
¾ cup lemon juice
¾ cup honey
¾ cup coconut oil (from health food store)
½ cup water
1 teaspoon vanilla extract
½ teaspoon salt

Citrus Date Sauce

7 pitted Medjool dates
1 tablespoon lemon juice

or

Cherry Sauce

½ cup pitted cherries
2-4 teaspoons honey

· For the crust, process the nuts in a food processor into a flour-like consistency. Add dates. Blend well. Press into a spring form pan.
· For the cheesecake, process cashews, water and lemon into a smooth texture. Add water, vanilla and salt. Bring honey and coconut oil to room temperature or clear liquid state by putting jars in several inches of boiling water for a few minutes. Then stream coconut oil and honey into mixture and process until smooth and thick. Pour on top of crust and tap until level and air bubbles are gone. Freeze for 2 hours or more. Let thaw and serve at refrigerator temperature.
· For sauce, blend ingredients in food processor until smooth. Add a small amount of water until sauce is desired consistency. Serve on the side or on top of cheesecake.

Trail of Whitewater Canyon

Drive up Whitewater Canyon, easy hike out to Red Dome
and moderate Canyon View Loop trail hike

ᝈ **Spicy Mint Green Smoothie**

❝Whitewater Canyon. What life is like without all the madness," said resident Charlotte Burns. "I've seen thirty or more bighorns on the cliffs that overshadow the lodge."

We were on our way to see for ourselves. The Interstate 10 freeway was ugly. There were fast moving clouds that darkened the sky. It had just rained. We took the Whitewater exit, turned north and drove 4.5 miles following the riverbank brightened by the yellow masses of spring blossoms on the brittlebush bushes.

Whitewater Canyon Visitor Center

We got out of the car at the visitor center parking lot. It was 8:30 a.m. and with the rain the temperature had dropped to 52 degrees. The small red building was unassuming, caught like debris in the meander of the Whitewater River and it was dwarfed by the yellow cliffs rising above it. T.M. opened the door and we stepped inside. It smelled good like wood. I looked at the stone walls, beautiful wood tables and in a smaller room just off the main room there was a gallery of landscape paintings. Morning light streamed through the windows. I held my hiking hat in my hand. "This could be the lobby of a five star hotel." T.M. said. The preserve manager was standing behind the desk.

He said, "It was once slated to become something like that."

He got out his map and using a pen traced an out and back trip to Red Dome and the Canyon View loop trail. When I asked about the bighorn sheep he said a while back he had gone up on the ridge with his camera before sunset and encountered a male bighorn. The near ninety minute staring contest with the ram ended when the sun went down. That story gave me goose bumps.

After T.M. and I had followed the peaceful riverbed out to a dark brick-colored hill of volcanic mud called Red Dome on a section of the Pacific Crest Trail, we doubled back for the more challenging climb up the Canyon View Loop trail bursting with yellow bush poppies.

The wind began to pick up. Then it began to gust so hard it slowed our progress up the ridge as we climbed 500 feet in less than a mile to a viewpoint. I squinted and looked out at the view. I couldn't believe my eyes. I had the sensation I was back hiking the Wicklow Mountains in Ireland or the Highlands in Scotland with the wind and the green rain-drenched mountains but we were standing at the portal to the San Gorgonio Wilderness, at the crossroads of the Sonoran and Mohave Deserts and at the cool moist edge of the coastal zone. That's a lot of diversity coming together and it was hard to take it all in. The river from this height was a white slash meandering its banks. The mountains were strong brown shoulders. The Coachella Valley desert sprawled out past the light tan foothills. The foggy clouds from the coast pressed into the pass. We began the climb down and felt the warm, dry desert air and smelled the aromatic white sage on the last leg of the loop.

Back at the visitor center we decided Charlotte was right. We were wind-burned, tired and relaxed. We didn't have a magical bighorn experience today but there was much to love about the beauty of the Canyon now that it was part of the Wild Lands Conservancy Sand to Snow Preserve. We took one last look behind us before we got on the 10 Freeway and into the chaos of modern life.

That week I told everyone, "Go hike Whitewater Canyon."

"You mean that freeway exit Whitewater?" they said.

"Yup. That one. And bring a jacket. It gets windy up there."

Travel notes

From Interstate 10 east of Banning and west of Palm Springs, take the Whitewater exit. Turn north then turn left on Whitewater Canyon Road. Travel 4.5 miles to the Whitewater Preserve located at the end of the road at 9160 Whitewater Canyon. Tip: Bring a jacket. Information: 760-325-7222 or www.wildlandsconservancy.org. The visitor center is open 8 a.m.–5 p.m. daily. Closed on Thanksgiving, Christmas, and New Years Day.

The well-marked trail to Red Dome begins on the north side of the parking lot. The trailhead marker is a large boulder. Head north, angle west across the riverbed on a plank/rope bridge. The trail meanders along the left edge of the river bed and at .5 mile joins the Pacific Crest Trail. Continue straight following the river bed out to Red Dome, a dark red outcropping on your left. You can continue on the PCT as far as desired. But for an easy 4.2 mile out and back trip with 400 foot elevation change return the way you came. This trail takes about 2 hours.

The Canyon View loop trail directions are the same as Red Dome but at the .5 mile junction with the PCT instead go left through the silver unlocked gate and climb the ridge with a 500 foot elevation change in .8 of a mile. At the top of the ridge make a left at the marked junction (if you go right you will stay on the PCT) Proceed along the ridge top. (There is a spur on your left to a high point overlook.) Continue south along the top of the ridge. The trail drops down to Whitewater Road. Go left about 100 yards, cross the river and at the yellow top post marker, proceed on the north side picking up the trail. Pass the visitor center then turn right and head back to the parking lot. This moderate 3.7 mile loop trail has a 1,158 elevation change and can be done at a leisurely pace in about 2.25 hours.

You can combine these 2 hikes by taking the Red Dome Trail out and back, then taking the Canyon View Loop Trail to return to the visitor center. This 8 mile moderate combination hike has an elevation change of 1,600 feet and will take about 4 hours.

Spicy Mint Green Smoothie

Recipe provided by Michael Miller, certified Gourmet Raw Food Chef and Instructor from Living Light Culinary Institute. He can be reached at www.lindampyle.com *Raw food is defined as a diet that is plant-based, consisting of fresh, ripe fruit, vegetables, nuts, seeds and sprouted grains.

¼ cup raw hulled sunflower seeds (soaked overnight, rinsed and drained)
4-6 mint leaves
⅔ cup spinach or kale leaves with stems removed
1 large ripe banana (speckled and brown)
½ cup blueberries
¼ teaspoon cinnamon
⅛ teaspoon cayenne pepper
1 cup purified water
½ teaspoon whole leaf Stevia green powder or 1 pitted date

· Combine ingredients in a blender. Optional: add 1 teaspoon bee pollen. Makes 1 serving.

Trail of the Fringe-Toed Lizard

Coachella Valley Preserve, Thousand Palms Oasis

ॐ Thousand Palms Heart of Palm Salad

Life is cool and easy at the Oasis straddling the infamous San Andreas fault line and the Indio Hills. The Fan Palms, tall monarchs of the desert, toss their green crowns. Benevolent shaggy skirts of thatch hide creatures from the sun. Pupfish swim in quiet pools. Carrizo grass drifts in the wind playing haunting flute sounds, an ancient song. Lounging fringe-toed lizards burrow into favorite sand dunes.

On the TRAIL OF THE FRINGE-TOED LIZARD, mountain biking the Indio Hills Trail is first on our itinerary and then a visit to the Thousand Palms Oasis and Visitor Center. But when we reach the trailhead off Dollar Road, we find it now designated Wilderness, closed to mountain bikers. Disappointed but happy to see its protected status and allowing for unforeseen setbacks, we head back to the Thousand Palms Oasis and change into hiking clothes.

Thousand Palms Oasis

The Coachella Valley Preserve straddles the San Andreas Fault and the Indio Hills. Water seeps along this earthquake rift, where faulting and fracturing make water available to the Thousand Palms Oasis. Hot and thirsty travelers in the past must have looked upon it as a miracle if not a desert mirage.

McCallum Grove Nature Trail

Descending into grotto-like coolness, T.M. and I begin the popular trail to the McCallum Grove. The sudden air-conditioned feeling is not just from the shade of the fan palms. Like an evaporative cooler, their huge leaves and dozens of other plant's leaves transpire water during the day. In the heart of the Oasis we feel ten or twenty degrees cooler than in the desert outside.

As we wind through the Oasis, I wonder what it would cost to own this oasis and how you could buy it? Eighty acres of Thousand Palms Canyon was worth just two mules and a wagon to Louis Wilhelm in 1906. His son, Paul Wilhelm, inherited it. Priceless now as the rare habitat of the palm oasis woodland, it is also home to the endangered Coachella Valley fringe-toed lizard, Uma inornata to his friends. The Preserve is jointly owned and managed by the Nature Conservancy, Bureau of Land Management, Wildlife Service, California Department of Fish and Game and California Department of Parks and Recreation.

Out of the sheltering heart of the Thousand Palms Oasis, in the sunlight, our feet clomp on boards over surface water of a salt grass marsh. Stopping to listen to a song coming from the marshy area, we learn it is the carrizo grass singing, peeping and squeaking as the wind rustles through it. Natives used the reeds from the thickets for thatching material and strong cordage.

Our self-guided tour brings us along a hot sandy stretch of trail and instructs us to stop and look down to observe the grinding of rocks into a fine powder. Under our feet the forces of the San Andreas Fault and its branches are at work; this powdery soil is associated with palm oases. A "linear zone of crushed rock and clay" acts as an underground dam inhibiting water flow and pushing it to the surface. Looking for water? Find it where fan palms pop up indicating water seeps, springs and steams. The lives of desert travelers in the past depended upon reaching oases such as these.

Above us, we witness what happens when the San Andreas Fault and parallel branches put the squeeze on the land. The bluff before us, once a enormous piece of alluvial fan, has been cleaved off and pushed up by this pressure.

Coachella Valley Preserve
McCallum Grove

After about a mile of walking, we reach the McCallum Grove, another cool Eden. Intrigued by the long skirts of thatch, I peek under the petticoat of an unmanicured fan palm knowing that although I see nothing, it is alive with oasis dwellers: black widow spiders, lizards, snakes, rodents and bats—all the creepy crawly things of human terror.

Another traveler's nightmare of the Coachella Valley desert is a persistent westerly wind. Wind, fitful and moaning, heavy laden with sand, can whip up mighty windstorms. But the blowing sand also creates sand dunes and sand shadows, a once prominent feature of this desert. Sand shadows are piles of sand on the sides of certain hills deposited when a wind losing its velocity drops its load of fine sand on the side of a hill.

On the round trip, T.M spots a lizard. Could it be a fringe-toe escaping predators and searing heat by burrowing under sand with a snout like a shovel? No, his stripes identify him as a cousin, the zebra striped lizard. Nicknamed the clown of the desert, he lifts his back end up like a scorpion and runs away teasing us to follow.

Reentering the deep dark of the Thousand Palms oasis, we picnic at a table near a screw bean mesquite tree. Inside the palm log cabin Visitor Center, the well-informed guide is helpful and shows us ancient shells perhaps from the time when the Sea of Cortez inundated the valley. When we ask about more local oasis history the guide remarks that it is hard to separate fact from fiction. The desert lends itself to tall tales with eccentric people telling of mysterious events.

As we leave, other trails in the Preserve call us to return to hike to the Indian, Pushawalla, Horseshoe, Hidden and Willis Palms Oases. Tomorrow's trails scouted, we head for downtown Palm Springs. Fan palms will not cool us there but manmade "misters" will.

Travel notes

To reach the Coachella Valley Preserve from the 1-10 Freeway go north on Monterrey .5 miles to Ramon Road. Go right on Ramon Road for 3.4 miles then go left at Thousand Palms Canyon Road. Proceed 1.9 miles and take a left into the parking lot. Parking lot hours are 7 a.m.-6 p.m. Visitor center information: 760-343-2733 or the Preserve office 760-343-1234 or www.coachellavalleypreserve.org.

The 2 mile out and back hike to the McCallum Grove will take about 1 hour.

Thousand Palms Heart of Palm Salad

The Cahuilla ate boiled "maul pasun" (heart of the palm) in times of food shortages. Today, hearts of palm, mostly from Brazil, come conveniently in a can.

One 14 ounce can heart of palm
6 tablespoons lemon juice
6 tablespoons olive oil
¼ cup red onion, finely chopped
12 ounces canned or fresh shrimp
½ teaspoon sea salt
Freshly ground pepper to taste
Romaine lettuce inner leaves
2 Haas avocados
Parmigiano Reggiano cheese

· Combine lemon juice, olive oil, onion, shrimp and salt. Add heart of palm cut into medium size chunks. Refrigerate for at least 2 hours. Just before serving place Romaine leaves on plate and spoon shrimp mixture on top. Sprinkle with diced avocado and fresh grated cheese. Serves 4.

Trail of Big Morongo Canyon

Bird watching and hiking the
Big Morongo Canyon Reserve trails

🍂 Tarragon Pine Nut Watercress Salad

The sight of water cress, water parsnip, wild tarragon and perennial Indian rhubarb growing along a trickling stream greets us as we meander along the willow-draped bird land of the Big Morongo Reserve. This is a place where the list of native plants reads like the ingredients for a gourmet tossed salad. We find a land of ample water and lush vegetation forming an important transition between the Mohave and Colorado Desert.

Big Morongo Reserve

On the TRAIL OF BIG MORONGO CANYON, we find the Reserve is named for the nomadic, powerful Serrano Indian clan, the Morongos, who inhabited the canyon long before the advent of white settlers.

Towering, rustling Fremont cottonwood trees stir memories of growing up in the Midwest. This symbolic tree of the arid West marks permanent sources of water and shade. The riparian forest that surrounds us is one of the ten largest cottonwood and willow oases in the California desert.

We start winding our way along Desert Wash and Willow Trail through fields of alkali golden bush warm in the sun. Although summer dry today, in the fall this blooming shrub is said to provide an ocean of golden color. Deeply rooted honey mesquite trees charred from a fire in the preserve in 1992 still show their sharp inch-long thorns.

A bird watcher's paradise, 1,400 pairs discreetly breed in these thickets. These riverside woodland and desert wash habitats have been documented to have the second highest per square kilometer density of breeding birds known in the United States. We listen for the "pit pitasee, pit pitasee," of the vermilion flycatcher. Hoping to see the flash of red scarlet of a male, we are disappointed and turn our attention back to the plants, especially the abundant wild tarragon.

Artemisia dracunculus, tarragon, draws its name from the ancient Roman world and a twig of this "little dragon" carried in a pocket protected from dragons and snakes. Picking our tiny olive-green talisman to protect us, we move safely on.

A 2-foot mass of parasitic plant hanging like a nest from many mesquite trees is desert mistletoe, toxic to humans but a fruit treat for the phainopepla bird. The mistletoe conceals a nest made of twigs, grass, flowers and leaves bound by spider web.

Along the Willow Trail, a boardwalk skirts the stream and we enter the cool canopy of red willows and white alders. Sitting on a listening bench, the sounds of bubbling water, unidentified birds and creaking trees are all to be heard.

Out in the sun, the Barn Loop Trail threads through a grassy field to a picturesque barn. The light sneaks into the old barn through missing boards, rests for a while on the floor and leaves to cross an old wheeled piece of farm equipment resting in the grass; wind rattles the boards. I had seen a 1920s picture of ranchers resting in the shade of the same tamarisk tree under which I stand.

After an hour of leisurely hiking and 41 stops on the trails identifying plants and habitats, we complete the Desert Wash, Willow and Barn Loop Trails, leaving Yucca Ridge, Mesquite and Canyon Trails to the busload of students arriving and plan to return on a fall day when the alkali goldenbush is in its full yellow glory.

Return in October

Greeted by golden alkali bush dressed in its best autumn gold, our return to the familiar preserve is a pleasure. Just as had been promised

Barn Loop Trail

photo credit: Evelyn McMillin

on the spring walk, the alkali goldenbush now dazzles—gold bullion against the blue sky.

We leave Mom and Dad to do the Yucca Ridge Trail where billion-year-old rock can be found. T.M. and I head down the Canyon Trail. They will drive our car to Indian Avenue allowing us a one-way hike.

Cottonwood trees rustle in the wind, a comforting sound; leaves sparkle in the sun as our feet crunch on an easy hike. Eventually the trail, a gentle downhill slope, becomes a wide road.

The trail meanders, winds and crisscrosses the stream. Rivers of gray rock run down the faces of steep canyon walls. I stop and touch the cold gray surfaces.

Leaving the somber canyon behind, we emerge to a spectacular stormy weather sight of purple Mount San Jacinto already dusted with crystalline snow; billowing white clouds drape its peak. The winds of a passing storm blow on the bajada as we finish the hike in 2 hours.

Later, rendezvousing with Mom and Dad, we inquire what the billion year old rock looked like? What rock they say? After a rocky ascent up to a bird's eye view of the surrounding Preserve, they turned back thinking they had missed the Yucca Ridge Trail and walked through the white dikes of feldspar intruding into ancient gneiss outcrops, completely oblivious to one of the oldest rock formations in California under their feet.

Travel Notes

To reach Big Morongo Canyon Preserve, take Interstate 10 to Highway 62 north to Morongo Valley. Proceed about 11.5 miles through the business district of Morongo Valley. Turn right on East Drive and go a short distance to the Preserve entrance on your left. Information: 760 -363-7190 or www.bigmorongo.org. Open daily 7:30 a.m. to sunset. Free but donations accepted. The Desert Wash, Willow and Barn Loop trails make an easy just over 1 mile loop which will take about 45 minutes. The easy Mesquite Trail to the moderate Yucca Ridge Trail is just over .5 miles and will take about 30 minutes. The 5.5 mile moderate Canyon Trail will take about 2.5 hours. For this hike leave one vehicle at the parking lot, and another at the lower end of the canyon. Park on the dirt road at the fenced pipeline facility several yards north of Indian Ave. about .5 miles east of Highway 62.

Tarragon Pine Nut Watercress Salad

The Indians ate watercress fresh in the spring or cooked it like spinach.

⅓ cup pine nuts
4 tablespoons olive oil
3 tablespoons lime juice
1 clove garlic
1 teaspoon chopped fresh tarragon
½ teaspoon sugar
Salt and pepper to taste
½ head Romaine lettuce
1 bunch watercress

· Toast raw pine nuts in a heavy bottomed shallow skillet stirring over a medium heat until lightly brown and fragrant. Set half aside.
· In food processor blend ½ nuts, lime, olive oil, garlic and sugar until smooth. Wash watercress, shake dry, grip bunch at neck and twist sharply to discard stalks.· Place watercress leaves and torn Romaine in bowl, toss with dressing and reserved nuts. Top each salad with freshly ground pepper. Serve with dark bread and date butter. Serves 2.

Date Butter

4 dates, chopped
½ cup butter
1 tablespoon orange zest
2 tablespoons honey

- Freeze dates for 10 minutes then chop finely in food processor. Add other ingredients to blend well. Makes about ½ cup.

Trail of the Joshua Tree

Oasis of Mara visitor center, drive to Split Rock,
short hike at Skull Rock, drive to Queen Valley,
short hike at Cap Rock and highlight hike in
Hidden Valley, Joshua Tree National Park

ঽ Big Rock Turkey and Artichoke Sandwich

M ists trail like gauzy scarves floating at the base of San Jacinto peak in Palm Springs. Miles away, day is dawning on Joshua Tree National Park, our destination where the rock is always the color of sunrise and sunset. Here strange human-like evergreen trees, as unusual as the landscape, dot the upper elevations.

On the TRAIL OF THE JOSHUA TREE, we wind through barren hills on Highway 62, Twentynine Palms Highway, climbing up to the Yucca Valley. Bringing the car to a screeching halt at the west entrance to the park in the town of Joshua Tree, we rethink our options to explore this expansive park stretching 60 miles east to west and 30 miles north to south, deciding to stick with our original plan to start at the Oasis Visitor Center in Twentynine Palms.

Oasis Visitor Center

The center is abuzz with some of the over one million visitors per year thumbing books and viewing displays. The names of visitors from Germany, Switzerland and the U.K. in the daily register show the international interest in Joshua Tree. President Franklin Roosevelt created the National Monument in 1936. In 1994, it was upgraded from a

Joshua Tree

Monument to a National Park and the Desert Protection Bill added 235,000 acres, most of it wilderness.

The Joshua Tree is a member of the agave family also related to the garlic and wild onion families. The tree we have come to see, this "great star of the desert," looks like a tree trunk with porcupines attached. Leathery leaves help it withstand the effects of the harsh elements of the desert: heat, wind and drought. Although looking very inhospitable, over two dozen species of birds nest or live in its uplifted branches.

With one of the park recommended guidebooks, Road Guide to Joshua Tree National Park, in hand we strike out leaving the hubbub of the Visitor Center to hike the ½ mile self-guided Oasis of Mara Nature Trail.

Oasis of Mara Nature Trail

The oasis trills with a sweet harmony of voices. Gambel's quail, robins, warblers and mourning doves form a twittering, peeping choir hidden by a tangled mass of green trees and fan palms. Mountains back the low ranch-style homes of the encroaching city of Twentynine Palms. The sibilant shush-shushing of palm fronds whispers the Serrano Indian lore of how the name Twentynine Palms came to be.

Indian women wanting to produce male children came to this "Oasis of Fertility" on the advice of their medicine man. They set up camp at this "little springs much grass" and as instructed planted a fan palm for each male child born. Twenty-nine trees were planted the first year. Quite a record.

The Oasis of Mara, with water rising to the surface along a section of the Pinto Mountain fault, formed a desirable environment for three native tribes, Serrano, Chemehuevi and Cahuilla. These peoples were known to have lived there hundreds of years before Anglos traced their foot trails into the desert.

Miners, homesteaders, cowboys and the stage line came later to the Oasis for water. We stand looking up at the god-forsaken mountains, bleak and barren and try to picture miners hauling barrels of water loaded onto horse-drawn wagons from the springs to their gold mining camps. Around 1873, a number of claims had been filed on lodes in the area. As the Oasis held the only water for miles around and water so necessary for processing of gold, a gold mill was located here.

Finishing our loop trail and back at the Center, we head out on the Utah Trail by car. The hills now become almost sandy, more eroded, no jagged peaks, some huge boulders. Extremes of temperature in this desperately dry desert can test man animal and plant to the limit. Plant leaves, stems and roots have adapted by shredding, shrinking and hoarding. Creosote bush, Mohave yucca and cholla cactus thrive at this elevation. The Joshua trees we seek need a higher elevation and we begin to slowly climb the alluvial fan to the high desert. At about 10 miles from the Visitor Center, we turn and travel one-half mile to a picnic spot at Split Rock.

Split Rock

Molten shapes of behemoth granite rocks of amber, champagne and ochre swallow us up. Serious rock climbers pass with their red backpacks, intent on scaling these formidable rock formations. But we choose a convenient picnic table to marvel at the strange titans strewing the landscape. I read to Mom and Dad with a mouth full of lunch about the formations around us and we realize we are sitting above huge rocks that were once oozing molten magma. Cooled, exposed and then peeled like an onion, layer by layer, by wind and the elements, these fantastic outcropping have become what we see today. Without this vital adaptation of rock to exposure to climate and breakdown to soil, terrestrial life on earth would be impossible. Lunch over, we scramble humbly up the rough surface of the tawny granite to see the cracked and split boulder that gave Split Rock its name.

Skull Rock

Driving a little more than a mile from our picnic area at Split Rock, we pull over to hike a portion of the Skull Rock Trail to Jumbo Rocks Campground all the time searching for the "Skull." On the trail our feet crunch on loose tiny pieces of rocks, the scaling of the enormous rocks around us. Joshua trees thrive in this particular soil.

We now know our pencil cactus from our jumping cholla and our Joshua tree from the Mohave yucca. But the learning comes slowly and the diversity of desert plants can be illusive. By keeping a discreet distance from the jumping cholla no viscous barbs hook our clothing.

We reach Jumbo Rocks campground where the bold outcrops of bedrock are more revealed evidence of tall castles of rock with their foundations far below in the underground, cooled and hardened 100 million years ago. Continuing erosion breaks down the peach-pink rocks and one can almost see their liquid, molten primal shape. In Africa, rock formations such as these are homes to lions but we see only one small lizard.

On an uncrowded trail marked with stones, we retrace our steps. Wild buckwheat, a low spreading plant, sports white flowers. The headache medicine the Indians made from this plant is one I could use right now. A Mohave yucca with purple-tinged flowers is alive with bees.

Back at the car, we lament to Dad that we have seen possible pears and coneheads in the jumble of rocks but not the "Skull." Turning to look once more, the eyeholes and protruding nose of a large rock are as plain as the nose on our faces. It is clearly marked with a huge sign on the road—the Skull.

Queen Valley

Our willing driver heads into Queen Valley. Soon we halt in the shade of a 30 foot blue-green Joshua tree to inspect it more closely. At its feet blooms a tiny rose-colored plant.

The Joshua tree can live to be a centenarian. The Indians ate the seeds and flowers said to have an unpleasant aroma reminiscent of mushrooms. Eons ago the extinct giant sloth browsed on the foliage, a staple in their diet. Flycatchers, flickers and woodpeckers have not shown today but two black ravens nest in the cradling arms of the

Joshua. Picturesque or grotesque depending on the viewer, the Joshua tree has come to symbolize the Mohave Desert.

Cap Rock

As a cold wind begins to pick up foretelling of a possible storm, we pass Ryan Mountain continuing on to Cap Rock. Dad, accompanying us on this paved Cap Rock Trail, looks back and notices he had parked beneath the little protruding rock forming the bill of Cap Rock. The signed trail, rambling through the rock cluttered landscape, is non-taxing and fascinating. Rock shapes reminiscent of sculptor Henry Moore's work recline on the valley floor. Here, in April, we are witness to the woolly daisy plant, just a tiny yellow bright face smiling up from its inhospitable space on the sand. The Mohave desert stars dressed in white create a fairyland garden.

Hidden Valley

Back in the car, passing the dirt road leading to Lost Horse Mine, we continue on to Hidden Valley. We start a 1-mile loop trail at the Hidden Valley picnic area. Entering a Zane Gray scenario, we slip between rocks through a narrow chasm into a pocket valley; a hidden highlight of the Park.

Grandmothers in shorts and scrambling children manage the trail very well. Mom squeezing through terra cotta rocks uses her hands to propel herself. A strange low wail of wind accompanies us as we thread our way between the many rounded rocks; scattered, they look as if they could have been shot out of canons by a battalion of giants. Underneath the wind, I hear the shouts of rock climbers, "Anyone want to check and go?" and "On belay." Climbers haul themselves over the brow of a rock tower using Joshua Tree National Park like an adult jungle gym. These adventure-seeking souls come to climb, conquer the rock and themselves.

Pressing through the many narrow crevices, thoughts of the cattle rustlers said to have used this concealed valley have us speculating as to just how they herded cattle through the tight spaces between rocks. Maybe the cattle were skinnier than those of today and more fit for leather than meat.

Legend says Jim McHaney, a disreputable cattle trader, kept horses and cattle of questionable brands in a clandestine corral here. Jim and his brother Bill, stock traders between Southern California and Arizona around the turn of the century, were said to have been so adept at rebranding that they sold stolen cattle back to unsuspecting original owners. Dangerous work in a day when cattle rustling and horse stealing was as serious as murder!

Tired, we exit the "real western" valley through a very narrow slit of rock to look out over a stand of Joshua trees lined up like an invading army of warriors. Arms raised, they seem ready to make an assault upon the rock-shooting giants of Hidden Valley.

We leave through the West entrance of the park and find ourselves in need of some caffeine in the town of Joshua Tree. The Cyberspace Café catches our eye. Inside, rock climbers drink malts and a woman talks to man about his mid-life crisis. A tall mysterious statue of a deer-man surveys the scene.

Driving down to Palm Springs, we drop to the Colorado Desert. Surreal rock formations give way to a vast panorama of the Coachella Valley. The rocky flanks of high mountains erode into gravel, sand, silt and salt filling the basins below. The floodwaters in the canyons spread this detritus into enormous alluvial fans. These fans from each canyon coalesce near the basin floor into a bajada, a notable feature of the desert floor.

Removing shoes from tired feet back down on the Valley floor, I notice a tiny piece of granite caught in the tread of my Nikes has hitchhiked with me. I remove it for safe keeping, knowing it to be a talisman that will bring us back to the Big Rock City, Joshua Tree National Park.

Travel notes

To reach the Oasis of Mara Visitors Center, from Palm Springs take Interstate10 to Highway 62 past the town of Joshua Tree and continue on to the town of Twentynine Palms. Turn right on National Park Drive (one block east of Adobe Road). The Oasis visitor center is open 8 a.m.-5 p.m. daily. Admission fee to the park is $15 and is good for seven consecutive days. Information: 760-367-5500

The Skull Rock nature trail is .25 miles. The Cap Rock nature trail is a .4 mile loop. The Hidden Valley nature trail is a 1 mile loop.

Big Rock Turkey and Artichoke Sandwich

1 pound loaf frozen bread dough
4 tablespoons olive oil, divided
1 medium onion, sliced
1 clove garlic, minced and divided
½ cup shredded carrots
1/3 pound fresh mushrooms, sliced
3 ounces marinated artichoke hearts, drained
½ pound turkey or chicken breast, sliced thinly
¼ pound hickory smoked turkey ham
½ cup Monterey Jack cheese, shredded
½ cup jalapeno cheese, shredded
1/8 teaspoon dried oregano
1/8 teaspoon dried basil

- Thaw dough until workable.
- Combine oregano, basil and ½ garlic with 3 tablespoons oil in shakable container and set aside.
- Sauté onions, ½ garlic, mushrooms and carrots in 1 tablespoon oil. Remove from oil. Pat artichoke hearts dry and slice thinly.
- Roll dough on unfloured board into a 14x10 inch rectangle. Place on greased baking sheet. Brush dough with herbed oil.
- Layer one-half side of dough with meats and vegetable mixture to within one inch of edge. Sprinkle on cheeses. Fold uncovered half of dough over layered side. Pinch edges together. Allow to rise 25 minutes. Prick tops. Brush with remaining herbed oil.
- Bake at 375 degrees Fahrenheit until light brown and hollow sounding when rapped. Cut into 2 inch slices. Serves 4–5.

Trail of Willie Boy

Drive to Landers and hike to the site of
Willie Boy Ambush and Memorial to Sheriffs

• Focaccia Sandwich

O ne "bad" outlaw Indian, Willie Boy, versus many "good" posse members. This scenario of high drama, worthy of a Western thriller, played out on Ruby Mountain against a Mohave Desert backdrop. On Ruby Mountain rocks are larger than life and conditions harder than most men can endure. Willie Boy country is still that way today, nearly a century later. But let's begin the TRAIL OF WILLIE BOY in the fall of 1909 when the West's last great manhunt began.

The Incident: Wife by Capture

Willie Boy, a young Paiute Indian known around Banning and Palm Springs as a good cowboy and a crack shot, lacked a key to Indian status—a wife. Lolita Boniface, a teenage Chemehuevi Indian girl, became his obsession in a plan to claim a wife by capture, an old Paiute tradition.

Late on a September night in 1909, Willie Boy stole up to forbidden Lolita asleep under a eucalyptus tree at Gilman's ranch. Winchester blasting, he killed her disapproving father at close range and held her family at gunpoint. Dragging the desired, resisting girl along, "Swift Fox" began his incredible 500-mile run.

Forming the Posse

The next day, inflamed by the murderous act and kidnapping, an 11-member posse including a Banning constable, a Riverside sheriff and 2 Indian trackers picked up their trail. Many had known the Earp brothers who grew up near Banning. Glimmers of glory perhaps fueled the manhunt.

Day 3: The Chase

Willie Boy had headed on foot for the open Mohave Desert. Indian knowledge led him to water seeps and rock water tanks. Lolita, barefoot and limping, soon became a cactus-scarred burden. Charlie Reche, foreman of the Desert Queen Mine, joined the hunt as the twelfth man.

Day 5: Lolita Found Dead

Still not even a glimpse of the fugitive. Then a gruesome find shocked the men; Lolita dead, face down on a granite slab with a bullet through her heart. A furor erupted when her bloodied body was carried back to town and displayed. As lurid reporting reached a fever pitch elevating Lolita to Indian princess and her father to Chief, the manhunt was quickly reinforced.

Day 8: Willie Boy Turns Back

Willie Boy had earned the respect of the posse who grudgingly marveled at his runs of up to 40 miles in one day and his uncanny ability to back-trail, eavesdrop and conceal himself behind nearly transparent creosote bushes, eluding even the Indian trackers. He slipped into his village, Twentynine Palms, for his stash of food and ammunition. It was gone. Running to within 75 miles of Nevada and freedom, inexplicably he turned back and headed toward his fate at Ruby Mountain.

Day 9: Hot on the Trail

The posse discovered a warm fire and concluded their ghost prey was close. Hot on the fresh trail in 100-degree heat, five of the men including Reche rode a frustrating 18 miles. Finally, horses exhausted, they stopped. Willie Boy still seemed as invisible as the wind.

Day 12: The Ambush

Reduced to eating raw chuckwalla by now, Willie Boy took the high ground on Ruby Mountain and waited in a fortified position.

Charlie Reche and the tired posse picked their way through the harsh canyon below him. Rifle shots rang out from above hitting some of the horses, scattering the men. But only Reche was hit. The bullet, deflected by metal handcuffs, wounded him but not fatally. Lying in the hot sun all afternoon, he played dead, while Willie Boy's fire held the posse at bay.

Willie Boy's rifle reverberated one more time. Then silence claimed the canyon. The men retreated after dark with wounded Reche.

Day 13: Reinforcing the Posse Again

The manhunt widened now to over 75 men and a legend was in the making. National reporters, bored with covering President Taft's visit to San Bernardino, picked up the story and wrote inflammatory articles inciting hysteria about an Indian uprising. A savvy Los Angeles Record reporter, Randolph W. Madison, chose to ride with the posse designated to go back to the site of the ambush at Ruby Mountain.

Day 16: Willie Boy's Fate

Madison's factual reporting and photographs documented the discovery of Willie Boy's bloated body, eye sockets starring into the sky, still in his last resting place on Ruby Mountain. Having discarded all his worldly possessions in a Paiute tradition, Willie Boy had fired his last bullet through his heart bringing his short life to an end. The posse had been chasing a ghost for many days.

Madison's camera recorded the somber lawmen linked forever in an image of the romantic but cruel West. Along with Willie Boy's body, cremated on a pyre of sagebrush on the spot where he was found, was burned the answers to all questions and the flames of legend and speculation were fanned anew.

Hollywood elevated Willie Boy to the status of an outlaw worthy of a legend of the West. For dramatic purposes, the story was fictionalized. The movie, *Tell Them Willie Boy is Here*, starring Robert Redford came out in 1969, the same year as Butch Cassidy and the Sundance Kid.

Chasing Willie Boy: Our First Attempt

Out in the middle of nowhere, we find ourselves on the Trail of Willie Boy barreling down a dirt road passing abandoned jackrabbit homesteads outside of Landers in search of the infamous Ruby Mountain, not knowing chasing Western myth and legend can be a difficult task. To track down the Willie Boy legend, we begin by exploring the high desert, the backdrop of the posses' chase. To see Willie Boy's sole ally, his only protector and weapon, the land and his Native American connection to it was important.

We wind up Highway 62 through Morongo Valley to Yucca Valley and on to Old Woman Springs Road, Highway 247. Local inquiry had told us to look for the church at New Dixie Mine Road. We turn up the dirt road with keen anticipation for the discovery of a real piece of Western history.

We stop and climb to the top of what seems to be the highest peak, Ruby Mountain, but find no memorial to posse or Willie Boy and retreat. Later T.M. is told by a local man who had led the annual Willie Boy Ride: "It didn't happen anywhere near Ruby Mountain, son."

Chasing Willie Boy: Our Second Attempt

Armed with our new information, we head out Old Woman Springs Road 6 months later. The weather has changed drastically and there is a good dusting of snow on San Gorgonio. White clouds leave black shadow stains, images of themselves, on the mountains. We turn up New Dixie Mine Road and climb past upland mesas and harsh canyons past Ruby Mountain. At 5,000 feet, one is close to the clouds and level with many mountain tops.

T.M. had warned it might be a jolting ride but it is fairly smooth. Up the canyon we rise gradually on a sandy rock-strewn jeep road, our competent driver keeping just the right speed to negotiate sand and rocks. Recent rain has brought blossoms to the woolly daisies and the brittlebush under Joshua trees. In this isolation, one can easily picture the story. Willie Boy running—running through this unforgiving land—running up to 40 miles a day leaving posse and horses spent.

At 6.7 miles down the dirt road, it bifurcates. On a small pipe is written Ambush Spring Road. Wilderness Designation prohibits

196

Cholla Cactus

farther road access by vehicle. Here we stop, have water and sandwiches in the car preparing for a pleasant hike. Dad and Mom decide definitely to stay in the sanctuary of the jeep. In this bleak wonderful landscape, they are not frightened but unwilling to risk hypothermia. Black clouds threaten to give a good gushing downpour at any time. T.M. and I strike out into the 49-degree temperature clad only in shorts and tee shirts.

The wind sweeping up the valley chilling us to the bone, we walk only 50 feet down the lonesome road before reluctantly acknowledging that Willie Boy has eluded us again and we are now only chasing the wind.

The 3-mile walk to the spot supposedly marking the final shootout becomes much too daunting in the fierce high desert wind. It took the sheriff's posse 16 days to find him. If it takes us three tries to reach the exact spot where it happened—so what!

Third and Final Attempt

One year after our second try, we head once more out the dirt road to Ambush Spring Road, certain today is the day. We have come on the same week in October in which Willie Boy died in 1909. A bobcat hightails it across the now familiar twisting road up the canyon. Mom and Dad are not with us but Dad said before we left, "Be sure and tell Willie Boy, hello, if you ever find him!"

Leaving the car behind, we begin the hike. Shadows still fall across the buckskin-colored road that quickly winds around a bend.

The morning Mohave sky burns like a clear blue flame. Silver spines, white-hot stars, gleam on cholla cactus. Deeply crevassed Joshua trees stand invulnerable to assaults of wind and sand. Bold domes of rock emerge from their subterranean strongholds. The savagery of the terrain is Wild West in all its glory.

Willie Boy grave and
Memorial to Sheriffs

T.M. out of sight, I feel the hot breath of a runner behind me and stop in my tracks. A quick glance over my shoulder has only Joshua trees and rocks staring back. Was it Swift Fox continuing his 500-mile run even now? Or was it only my own footfalls and breathing, unfamiliar in the silence of the desert?

My own questions unanswered, too soon it seems, T.M. shouts: "I've found it, it's here, over the rise." WILLIE BOY 1881-1909 THE WEST'S LAST GREAT MANHUNT is the inscription on the gravestone embedded in rock.

A chain link fence protects the small white boulder next to which he was found. Shot gun shells lay on the ground. Vandals have shot up a wooden sign reading "Willie Boy Grave". We compare Madison's pictures of the posse with rifles on shoulders standing over Willie Boy. The rocks match up exactly.

The warm October wind blows from the northeast as we peer down into the canyon below. Nearly invisible spider webs crisscross low blackbrush plants surrounding the rocks I sit on as I play out the ambush. The posse came up the canyon from the north. Would the sun have been in the posse's eyes? We can only speculate why Willie Boy came back to face down the posse but it makes the myth complete, the story a legend.

This classic clash of white man and Indian had another character we had now come to know—the formidable and illusive Mohave Desert. We cannot know the Paiute ways or what was in the hearts of the posse but we can know the desert as they would have experienced it.

Time to leave but I want to linger savoring the empty desolate silence and the stark beauty. Why had I been obsessed with finding this place? T.M. said it was rewarding because it took three tries but it was more than that. Walking back down Ambush Spring Road to the car I knew the answer. It was the place where the Trail of this book would end.

Willie Boy and I had each chosen to end our journeys here on a crisp fall day in October under the blue Mohave sky where the rocks are larger than life and conditions harder than most men can endure.

There are numerous differing accounts of the Willie Boy affair. Questions are raised about who killed Lolita and if Willie Boy really died. One book by Harry Lawton, Willie Boy, explores the legend by interviewing the surviving posse, researching Indian bureau reports and separating fact from tabloid fiction. For the extensive details of the manhunt, maps and historic photographs this is an excellent book.

Travel notes

From Interstate 10 take Highway 62, 21 miles north to Yucca Valley. at Old Woman Springs Road (Highway 247) turn left. Pass Reche Road and at 11.1 miles take a left at the Landers Community Church onto New Dixie Mine Road. The unpaved road is suitable for high clearance vehicles only. Proceed 6.6 miles and bear right at the fork. Go right again on Ambush Spring Road and at 6.7 miles park. Proceed on foot as the road is now designated Wilderness. The memorial is approximately 3 miles down Ambush Spring Road and easily found. The 6 mile hike will take about 2.5-3.5 hours.

Focaccia Sandwich

1 package refrigerated pizza dough
¾ cup spaghetti sauce
¾ cup finely diced sausage or pepperoni, lightly sautéed
1 cup mozzarella or Monterey Jack cheese, diced
1 teaspoon oregano

· Remove dough from package. Unroll on unfloured breadboard. Stretch carefully into a 10x12 inch rectangle making sure center is not too thin. Spread on in order, sauce, meat and cheese, to an inch from edges. Roll tightly starting on longer end. Punch cut ends down the center with knuckles and pinch ends together. Place cut end down on greased baking sheet. Bake for 5 minutes in 400 degrees Fahrenheit oven. Reduce to 375 degrees Fahrenheit and bake until well browned 10–15 minutes longer.

Remove from oven. While cooling pinch together any breaks in dough. Cut into 1–½ inch slices when cool.

To thank you for purchasing Peaks, Palms & Picnics Linda is offering a **FREE EXCLUSIVE GIFT**

To register go to her website **www.lindampyle.com**
Choose any one of the following bonuses:

1. A free hiking consultation with Linda

2. T.M.'s *Ten Essentials of Hiking*

3. Linda's color photos of common desert plants to print and carry along on the trail for identification

4. More delicious recipes

5. Sample chapters from her upcoming book, *Awesome Day Journeys-Palm Springs*.

Linda would love to hear from you about your adventures on these trails. Contact her at
lindapyle@cox.net

Linda's Current and Upcoming Books

Pacific Peaks & Picnics
Day Journeys in San Diego County
$15.95 ISBN 0-916251-66-7
Order online: www.sunbeltbooks.com
Sunbelt Publications 800-626-6579
www.amazon.com
www.bn.com
www.borders.com

Awesome Day Journeys — Palm Springs
Linda Pyle's follow up to **Peaks, Palms & Picnics**.
More awesome hikes, walks and visits in and around the
mountains and deserts of Palm Springs.

Dawn Breaks in the West
A historical fiction novel of love, loss and triumph as a young
doctor from the east lands in Palm Valley (Palm Springs) after she
has fled the battlefields of the American Civil War.

Meditations in an Emergency, Tuscany, Italy
Walking in Saint Catherine of Siena's Italy.

Index of Recipes

Butter

Breads

Sandwiches

Salads

*Denotes Raw food recipe

References And Suggested Reading

Ainsworth, Katherine, *The McCallum Saga*, 1996, Palm Springs
Public Library

Batterson, Mark and Boddie, William, Salt, *The Mysterious
Necessity*,—, Dow Chemical

Bogart, Frank, *Palm Springs First Hundred Years*, 1987, Palm Springs
Heritage Associated

Bowart W.H., Hector, Julie, McManus Sally Hall, Coffman, Elizabeth
Kiely, *The McCallum Centennial*, for the Palm Springs Historical
Society, Reprint from Palm Springs Life Magazine

Bowers, Janice Emily, *Shrubs and Trees of the Southwest Deserts*,
Southwest Parks and Monuments Association, 1993

Bean, Lowell and Lawton, Harry, *The Cahuilla Indians of Southern
California*, 1997, Malki Museum Press

Bean, Lowell John and Saubel, Katherine Siva, Temalpakh, *Cahuilla
Indian knowledge and usage of plants*, 1972, Malki Museum Press

Bean, Lowell John, Brakke, Sylvia Vane and Young, Jackson, *The
Cahuilla Landscape*, 1991, Ballena Press

Bright, Marjorie Belle, *Nellie's Boardinghouse*, 1981, ETC Publications

Brumgardt, John R. and Patterson, Tom, *The Bradshaw Trail:
Narrative and Notes*, —, Historical Commission Press

Chase, J. Smeaton, *Our Araby, Palm Springs and the Garden of the
Sun*, 1987, Republished by the City of Palm Springs Board of
Library Trustees

Clark, Jeanne L., California *Wildlife Viewing Guide*, 1996, Falcon
Press

Decker, Barbara and Robert, *Road Guide to Joshua Tree National
Park*, 1994, Double Decker Press

Fitzgerald, Edward, *The Rubaiyat of Omar Khayyam,*—, Illustrated Editions Company

Green, Michael, *Patton's Tank Drive, D-Day to Victory,* 1995, Motorbooks International

Jackson, Helen Hunt, *Ramona,* 1912, 1939, Little Brown and Company

James, George Wharton, *Wonders of the Colorado Desert,* 1911, Boston Little, Brown, and Company

Jaeger, Edmund C., *Desert Wild Flowers,* 1940, 1941, Stanford University Press

Jorgensen, Mark, *The Plight of Anza-Borrego's Desert Bighorn Sheep,* Jan 1998, www.desertusa.com

Kotzen Alice, *Malki Museum's Native Food Tasting Experiences,* 1996,—

Little, Elbert L., *National Audubon Society Field Guide to North American Trees,* 1980, Alfred A. Knopf

Lawton, Harry, *Willie Boy, A Desert Manhunt,* 1960, Malki Museum Press

Mancini, Richard, *American Legends of the Wild West,* 1992, Quintet Publishing Limited

May, Antoinette, *A Lonely Voice of Conscience,* 1987, Chronicle Books

Meier, Jim, *Last Rites for a Desert Bighorn,* March 1998, www.desertusa.com

Muench, Jon, *The Plight of Anza-Borrego's Desert Bighorn Sheep,* Feb. 1998, www.desertusa.com

Mile, Corcourtney, *Sacred Places in North America, A Journey to the Medicine Wheel,* 1994, Stewart, Tabori and Chang

Norris, Robert M. and Webb, Robert W., *Geology of California,* 1990, John Wiley and Sons

Pepper, Choral, *Guidebook to the Colorado Desert of California,* 1974, Ward Ritchie Press

Pyle, Ernie, *Ernie Pyle's Southwest,* 1935, Desert Southwest Inc.

Robinson, John, *San Bernardino Mountain Trails,* 1986, Wilderness Press

Ross, Delmer G., *Gold Road to La Paz, An Interpretive Guide to the Bradshaw Trail,*—, Tales of the Mojave Road

Sayre, April Pulley, *Desert,* 1994, Twenty First Century Books